The
SHRINK
and the
SAGE

The
SHRINK
and the
SAGE
A Guide to Living

JULIAN BAGGINI
ANTONIA MACARO

ICON

Published in the UK in 2012 by
Icon Books Ltd, Omnibus Business Centre,
39–41 North Road, London N7 9DP
email: info@iconbooks.com
www.iconbooks.com

Sold in the UK, Europe and Asia
by Faber & Faber Ltd, Bloomsbury House,
74–77 Great Russell Street,
London WC1B 3DA or their agents

Distributed in South Africa by
Jonathan Ball, Office B4, The District,
41 Sir Lowry Road, Woodstock 7925

Distributed in Australia and New Zealand
by Allen & Unwin Pty Ltd,
PO Box 8500, 83 Alexander Street,
Crows Nest, NSW 2065

Distributed in Canada
by Publishers Group Canada,
76 Stafford Street, Unit 300
Toronto, Ontario M6J 2S1

ISBN: 978-184831-377-4

Typeset in Minion by Marie Doherty

Printed and bound in the UK
by Clays Ltd, St Ives plc

CONTENTS

CONTENTS

Part Two

Julian Baggini is founding editor of *The Philosophers'* *Magazine* and the author of numerous books including *The Pig That Wants to be Eaten* and *The Ego Trick*.

Antonia Macaro has many years' experience as an existential therapist and philosophical counsellor, and is the author of *Reason, Virtue and Psychotherapy*.

INTRODUCTION

Everyone with the slightest jot of wisdom, from the Buddha to the jaded old soak behind the bar, would ruefully nod in acquiescence with writer and broadcaster Garrison Keillor's line: 'Life is a struggle, and if you should feel really happy, be patient: this will pass.' No wonder that the marketplace in life guidance is so crowded with both buyers and sellers. Canny shoppers might reasonably conclude: nothing works.

But while it's true that no *thing* works, some *things* work. There is no secret, magic formula, no algorithm for living a good, satisfying life. But in the accumulated wisdom of the generations there are ideas and practices that can help us to deal with the problems of living that come as the non-negotiable fee for the privilege of being born. If we can use them well, we can develop practical wisdom: the ability to think for ourselves and make better choices about how to live.

There is a huge risk of hubris in daring to write about such matters. But by doing so we do not make any claims about our own wisdom. One of the features of practical wisdom is that you can't tell how much of it people have by finding out what they know. Just as a clever mechanic can accomplish more with a single screwdriver than an incompetent one with a fully-equipped garage, so a little knowledge can go a long way for a wise person, while a lot can be wasted on a fool. All we claim is that we have access to a well-stocked garage, which we invite you to visit and use as you see fit.

Our toolkit is equipped with the resources of both psychotherapy and philosophy. It might not quite look as you'd expect. In particular, there is a widespread perception that both psychotherapy and philosophy are centrally concerned with exposing hidden depths. Philosophy pulls back the veil of appearances and reveals the real world for what it is, while psychotherapy is mainly an exploration of the unconscious. But while it is the case that some truths lie buried and things are often not as they seem, there is no reason to systematically concentrate on the invisible rather than the visible. In therapy, for instance, the reasons people give for their behaviour are often more illuminating than speculation about motives they might not be aware of.

We offer no grand unified theory. Our perspectives, tools and insights were gleaned from centuries-old philosophy and recent research in psychology. They also reflect the experience, over many years, of talking to people who were trying to work out how to live, and reflecting on those conversations. But although we draw from many sources, it's very important to us that what we say fits into a coherent framework. We have striven to avoid the kind of promiscuous pick-and-mix approach that ends up with a hodgepodge of incompatible, contradictory advice from different thinkers and systems.

We would describe our overall ethos as a minimalist one: while we believe that we can do things to make life better, solve some problems and make others less debilitating, we do not believe that lasting, uninterrupted contentment is a reasonable goal, even if some people do manage to achieve it. We hope and believe our resources can be of help, but they will not solve all your problems because life's problems are just not like that.

In Part One we scrutinise twenty potentially tricky spheres of life. In Part Two we each explain a little about our approach. But before getting going we thought it would be useful to outline the central ideas of the philosopher and psychologist who has most influenced our thinking about problems of living: Aristotle. His work is a rare find when it comes to questions of how to live. Although he wrote over two thousand years ago, lacking all kinds of knowledge we now take for granted (and of course getting some things completely wrong as a result), his understanding of being human is more insightful and relevant than many modern theories. We have both taken much inspiration from his framework for the good life, and his influence can be seen behind every page of this book. We hope that filling in some of the background to our perspective will help to illuminate both the connections between the topics we discuss and any questions we don't cover within these pages.

If you want to know more, give Aristotle's *Nicomachean Ethics* a go. It's essentially a set of lecture notes and so you may need to join a few dots, but we believe it's well worth the effort, as this is one book that really merits the over-used tag of 'essential reading for everyone'.

Although this book has two voices, they are intended to be in harmony, complementing more than contrasting with each other. Whether or not they're singing the right tune is for you to decide.

THE WAY OF ARISTOTLE

Practical wisdom

To say Aristotle was a philosopher is an understatement. He was arguably the greatest polymath who has ever lived. As well as writing some of philosophy's foundational texts on abstract matters of logic and metaphysics, he also turned his mind to biology, drama and the ordering of human affairs. His ability to seamlessly move from the abstract to the concrete is nowhere more evident than in his writings on ethics, and is encapsulated in an idea he put at the centre of a good human life: practical wisdom, *phronēsis*. If we have this we'll reliably come up with the right judgements about how to act in different situations.

The question is, how do we go about developing it? First of all we need to think through our values and reach a good awareness of the sorts of things that contribute to a good life. Then it's a question of gaining the skills to put this understanding into practice. These include thinking clearly about ourselves, our situation, other people, what is and is not possible; sharpening the ability to select and assess potential goals, work out the best way to achieve them, monitor their consequences, and use what we learn to adapt and change.

But good decision-making is only the first step. It's just as important that the appropriate actions flow from it without too much struggle. Pushing ourselves to stick to our deliberations while gritting our teeth is better than not implementing them at all, but the ideal is to be able to follow them gracefully and easily. Reason will still have to guide this process, however, by instigating the actions and habits that can help us to develop the relevant qualities and character traits. This is how we become more likely to do the right thing automatically, without having to cogitate at every turn.

There is nothing mystical or mysterious about this ability. Aristotle's ideas have a striking parallel in contemporary psychology's concept of expert intuition. Once you've become an expert in any field, the best course of action is liable to pop up without the need to articulate the exact reasons behind it. Of course your judgement is always fallible, and it's good practice to try to work out the rationale for it. Nonetheless, explicit justification often comes after the event, which is just as well, since we often have to rely on experts to make good decisions quickly. In this sense practical wisdom is simply expertise in the art of living.

Developing practical wisdom is not easy, but Aristotle has a useful device to think about it. It's the *doctrine of the mean*. The idea is that we are not faced with a binary choice to be, say, assertive or unassertive, courageous or timid, hedonistic or puritanical. Instead, we have to find a place on a scale that is appropriate for us and the situation we're in. That place is called the mean. This is how Aristotle puts it:

For example, fear, confidence, appetite, anger, pity, and in general pleasure and pain can be experienced too much or too little, and in both ways not well. But to have them at the right time, about the right things, towards the right people, for the right end, and in the right way, is the mean and best; and this is the business of virtue. Similarly, there is an excess, a deficiency and a mean in actions.[1]

But the mean is not bland moderation for all. We shouldn't always aim at a modest amount of anger: some situations might call for great anger (although how it's expressed is another matter) and others for none at all. The mean should be finely calibrated to our particular circumstances. Aristotle is very clear about this, explicitly stating that the mean for human action is not like a mathematical average. Take weight, for example. 50kg is too light for a six-foot man and 100kg too heavy. But the mathematical average – 75kg – is not necessarily the right one for any given individual. A slight-framed dancer may need to be lighter, a body-builder closer to the excess. As with much else in the good life, there is no algorithm for calculating the mean.

Maybe we don't think about it in these terms, but many life issues we find difficult are struggles to find the mean. We may want to take more risks, be more confident, more patient, more tenacious, more able to resist immediate gratification. We may wonder whether we are pushing ourselves too hard or not hard enough, at what point tolerance gives way to being a doormat or courage to recklessness, what the right balance is between achievement and enjoyment. This dynamic is evident in many of the problems of living discussed in this book.

At times the mean is hard to locate, and Aristotle gives us two rules of thumb to deal with those situations. One is to steer away from the more harmful extreme. When you see the sign warning of bears, is it cowardly to turn back or appropriately brave to carry on? If you're really not sure, turn back: better to have missed out on a lovely walk than to be mauled to death by an angry grizzly. The other is to steer away from the extreme towards which we are naturally inclined. In any sphere of human behaviour most of us tend more towards one pole. If you are inclined to be excessively cautious, say, you can gently nudge yourself towards the mean by taking tiny steps to be slightly more daring.

Moving towards the mean is possible because, unlike other objects in the universe, human beings have the capacity to change. As Aristotle put it, 'a stone that naturally falls downwards could not be made by habituation to rise upwards, not even if one tried to habituate it by throwing it up ten thousand times ... nor anything else that naturally behaves in one way be habituated to behave differently'. In contrast, good settled dispositions, which Aristotle calls *virtues*, 'arise in us neither by nature nor contrary to nature, but nature gives us the capacity to acquire them, and completion comes through habituation'.[2]

We are responsible for building our character despite the deep roots of our behaviour in our childhood experience (and, we would now add, genetic inheritance). But how can we effect these changes? Primarily through *habituation*. 'We become builders by building, and lyre-players by playing the lyre', wrote Aristotle. 'So too we become just by doing just actions, temperate by temperate actions, and courageous by courageous actions.'[3] Again, Aristotle's ancient insight finds itself vindicated by contemporary psychological research. Various forms of behaviour therapy work precisely because changing what you do can influence how you think and feel.

The aim of all this self-training is not unthinking automaticity, but the intertwining development of our rational deliberation and our immediate responses. Aristotle's account of the interplay between instinct and reflection has similarities with 'dual-process' models of the brain, such as the one described by psychologist Daniel Kahneman. This describes two systems: System 1 is concerned with fast, automatic, unconscious thinking, System 2 with slow, conscious deliberation.[4] Although Kahneman points out that the latter has little direct control over the former, it seems evident that reason can exert indirect influence on some instinctive reactions, for example by initiating habit change.

This does not happen without friction. If we have a habitual inclination to be impatient, say, and decide to cultivate patience, initially our only option may be to go against the grain and control our behaviour, suppressing the impulse to butt in, move on or give up. But if we persevere, eventually we should come to *feel* as well as *act* appropriately. We have achieved *virtue* or *excellence* (*aretē*) when inclination and deliberation feed harmoniously into each other.

The good life

Practical wisdom includes a good understanding of what is valuable in life. You cannot judge where the mean lies between cowardice and bravery, for instance, unless you are clear whether and how much something is worth taking a risk for. The right degree of loyalty will vary depending on how important you think it is to maintain social and family ties when other considerations suggest they should be severed. Any verdict about what it is best to do implies a judgement about what kind of life is better or worse.

We tend to be suspicious of general pronouncements about how best to live, often preferring to see these choices as purely subjective. But it wouldn't be surprising if some elements of the good life were more or less universal, given the many experiences that all humans share. At the very least we should all be able to agree that a good human life is bound to look different from a good life for a cat or a pig. Rolling in mud may be fun sometimes, but doing it as much as a pig is no way for a human to live.

Trying to identify one or a set of key ingredients for the good life has been a kind of philosophical parlour game for millennia, over which time the key contenders have remained pretty constant. Richard Layard, for instance, believes there are strong evidential grounds for identifying five factors as being the most important for happiness: family relationships, financial situation, work, community and friends, and health. Although Aristotle is interested in flourishing rather than happiness (see 'The problem with happiness' in Part One), he starts his discussion with some of the same usual suspects.

Unlike many other philosophers of his time, Aristotle thought that some material comfort was a suitable part of the good life, since 'human nature is not self-sufficient for contemplation, but the body must be healthy and provided with food and other care'.[5] But money, like health, is only a means to an end, and so he quickly dismisses it as a life-guiding goal. We shouldn't waste our life amassing material possessions, which we could lose at any point anyway, at the expense of more worthwhile goals. We can make the best of even unfortunate circumstances, just like 'a shoemaker makes the noblest shoe out of the leather he is given'.[6]

As for achieving fame or reputation, a common goal of our times, it can't be the main life pursuit either, according to Aristotle. Not only is it too dependent on other people and the workings of chance, it's also too indiscriminate. We'd be wrong to want recognition for its own sake, since it's not the honour that really matters, but receiving it from good people for our true good qualities.[7]

Good relationships have been widely identified by psychologists as important for well-being. Unfortunately when such studies are reported they tend to focus on quantity rather than quality, suggesting that there is an ideal number of friends we should have. One study suggested that the number of friends a person has at school is a good predictor of future wealth, with every extra friend adding 2 per cent to adult earnings.[8] Aristotle is very sensible about this, saying we'd be hard pushed to describe someone who is totally solitary as having a good life: 'no one would choose to live without friends, even if he had all the other goods'.[9] A good life should include other people, and especially solid relationships based on genuine mutual admiration, rather than merely pleasant or useful ones. However, a good person also 'wishes to spend time with himself',[10] partly because 'the wise man can contemplate even when he is by himself' and so is 'the most self-sufficient'.[11] Important though they are, good relationships with others facilitate rather than constitute the good life.

Aristotle also considers pleasure. He starts with the austere statement that people whose main interest lies in bodily pleasures live lives that are 'fit only for cattle'.[12] Nonetheless, he ends up defending an appropriate degree of pleasure along various lines. First of all, even purely bodily pleasures are good in moderation. We are embodied creatures, and too little appreciation of bodily pleasures can hinder our quest for the good life. It's only excessive indulgence that is damaging and distracts us from more interesting pursuits.

He also points out that there are different kinds of pleasures, and the best kind derives from being involved in a worthwhile activity. This can sound like high-minded prejudice. Just like when in the nineteenth century John Stuart Mill distinguished the higher pleasures of art and intellect from the lower pleasures of the body,[13] there is a suspicion that philosophers try too hard to justify their preferred pleasures over those of *hoi polloi*. But this is less a matter of mind versus body than intellectual engagement versus passivity. Think, for instance, of listening to music. You could just let it wash over you, or you could attend to it consciously, appreciating its qualities. In the first case, your pleasures are more animal or child-like; in the second, they are distinctively human.

While the example is not particularly Aristotelian, the distinction is, and it's a key one. Each type of living thing has its own nature or function, and the good life for any-thing means living in accordance with that. So the good life for human beings involves living in accordance with our nature as rational animals. There are two reasons why this may sound implausible. The first is that we have become more sceptical about the idea of human nature, let alone that of a natural 'function'. The second is that to place rationality at the centre of human life seems a bit elit-ist and naive. Aren't we much more affected by irrational impulses than rational ones?

Aristotle may have overstated the extent to which humans are rational. He did nevertheless give due weight to our embodied nature, while insisting that it should be governed by rationality. The parts of us that are in common with other animals are not denied or suppressed, simply not left to run the whole show.

As for human nature, it need not be understood as something strictly fixed and tied to a notion of our proper function. To say that a good life is one lived in accordance with our nature simply means that it is lived in ways that most fully bring out our potential to live as more than just animals. This involves using reason, but not necessarily in some high-minded, scholarly way. Practical wisdom, as we have seen, lies at the heart of Aristotle's vision for the good life, and that is something we can all develop, no matter what our academic aptitude. We can talk of human reason in a broad sense, in contrast to simply following instincts unthinkingly.

While Aristotle had some specific views that might seem too prescriptive – he is widely considered to have believed the best kind of life to be contemplative at its core, for instance – his framework is fundamentally pluralistic. This means it can be filled out in different ways, since there are many routes to a distinctively human life. Whether a life is centred on science, art, sport, craft, comedy, or altruism to strangers, it's a life no other animal can live, not even a chimpanzee or a dolphin.

An essential part of what it means to be human is to have the capacity to deliberate and make choices for ourselves, and no one can provide us with easy answers about what we should do. What we need, and what Aristotle provides, is not a set of prescriptions that diminishes our responsibility to make our own choices, but a philosophy of life that provides a framework for making better ones.

Part One

Part One

BEING THE BEST YOU CAN

The Shrink

⟿⟿

Imagine being the best possible version of yourself. What would you do? Would you be more confident, tolerant, sociable, go-with-the-flow? Would you sport an impressive knowledge of opera, or nineteenth-century Russian literature? Become a nonchalant polyglot? Climb the highest rungs of your career ladder?

The idea that we should perfect ourselves in some way is deeply engrained in the fabric of our times. Many books are dedicated to self-improvement. Not that it's always clear how to go about it. It used to be more straightforward. For Samuel Smiles, who published *Self-Help* in 1859, people should develop the high-minded qualities of application, perseverance and thrift. Now it's a bit all over the place, and self-improvement can legitimately include wine appreciation. And the advice is often contradictory: do we improve ourselves by learning to express our emotions, for instance, or to control them?

Similarly, fulfilling our potential is such an imperative that a feeling of not living up to it can come to haunt even the most accomplished. Then we are liable to blame ourselves for the gap we perceive between what we think we would be capable of and what is in fact happening in our lives. We imagine that with a little more foresight or application we really could have perfected all our potentialities.

While the impulse to be a better person is nothing but admirable, our thinking about it can go wrong in many ways. Perhaps the worst error is becoming too obsessed with the pursuit of perfection. It's not uncommon to fear that if we let go of this ideal we'll sink into a sloppy carelessness, just doing the least we can get away with. At the same time we might wonder whether it's worth sacrificing our sanity on the altar of high standards. But does it really have to be one or the other? Perhaps it's our dichotomous thinking that is the problem: perfection or mediocrity; either we always achieve the highest standards or we're a failure.

Albert Ellis, founder of Rational-Emotive Behaviour Therapy (REBT), wrote persuasively about the dogmatic and absolute musts with which we torment ourselves. The belief that in order to be a worthwhile person we must have 100 per cent success, for instance, is neither rational nor helpful. Perfection is not something a human being can achieve. And the more we cling to the demand that we *must* succeed the less likely we are to do so. It can be paralysing to think too much about end results.

As often, the Stoics have bequeathed us some useful advice: if we take archery as a metaphor, the idea is that we should do our best to shoot as skilfully as we can, but we can never guarantee we'll hit the bull's-eye. The aim of shooting well is in our power; but once the arrow has left the bow it's outside our control. We wrongly imagine we should be able to control outcomes when all we can control is our effort.

Paradoxically, self-improvement cannot survive without acceptance of imperfection and tolerance of failure. Without this softening influence, a concern for betterment can easily turn into a narcissistic focus on oneself, or a self-critical perfectionism.

Another potential mistake is to take too much responsibility for what we make of ourselves. Don't get me wrong: taking responsibility is good. It allows us to take steps to change things. But it would be unfair to ourselves not to take the situation into account. We don't exist in a vacuum, and our circumstances can be more or less conducive to flourishing. In a different context we might have been able to develop certain talents and qualities a lot more, but perhaps the conditions were not right for them to grow in the life we actually had.

Finally, we can focus too much on the failures, on what is left unfulfilled. We have to accept that self-improvement can never encompass all aspects of our lives, and that tending some potentialities inevitably means letting others wilt. We have limited resources, and it's not always possible to devote our energies to all tasks equally. Many high achievers, for instance, will readily admit they haven't become the best human beings, friends, or partners they could have been. We can never be the best we can in every aspect of our life. That is just part of the human condition.

But loss in one direction may well mean gain in another, and we could choose to pay attention to the potential we did develop instead. You may have left your athletic or business potential unfulfilled but gained a rewarding domestic life, or vice versa. Given our limitations, we should think carefully about what we're going to invest energy in. It's good to try to boost our memory, say, but if we allocate too much of our resources to it there will be a cost in lost opportunities or deterioration somewhere else.

Of course none of this means we should enthusiastically embrace imperfection as an excuse not to make an effort. But only if we accept imperfection will we be able to treat ourselves and others kindly when success is elusive.

The ideal to be the best we can be should be seen as just that: an ideal. So we should concentrate on doing the best job we can while fully appreciating the inevitability of imperfection. Japanese psychiatrist Shoma Morita, founder of Morita Therapy, came up with a catchy version of this thought with his advice to 'be the best imperfect person you can be'.

Any nagging feelings of dissatisfaction about unfulfilled potential can be constructively interpreted as implicit statements of value. Expressing a need or desire to develop certain areas of our life in ways we have so far neglected, they can help us to steer our actions towards a different, more fulfilling course. But in this as in many other cases, the direction of travel matters more than the finishing line.

The Sage

In the 1920s, French psychologist Émile Coué argued that by reciting the mantra 'Every day, in every way, I'm getting better and better' we could, by the power of suggestion, make it come true.[14] Whether or not such techniques have the desired effect, surely it would be wonderful if they did. How could it ever be worse to be better?

The thought of, say, someone practising air guitar 24/7 should be enough to challenge any assumption that too much improvement is a contradiction in terms. When it comes to being better people, some progressions matter more than others.

Consider, for instance, the difference between what we might call the moral life and the flourishing life. To improve morally is to treat others better and have a more positive impact on the world. To flourish is for your life to go better for you: healthier, full of richer experiences and deeper relationships. In pursuit of this second kind of improvement we tend to focus on what provides the most gain for us: losing weight, learning a new language, controlling our tempers and so on.

What I find interesting, however, is that people often justify these projects by pointing to their altruistic dimensions. When we become better we become more interesting, genial people to be with, they say. Even with that most narcissistic of goals, personal happiness, people will cite evidence that happier people tend to be more generous, sympathetic and caring towards others.

There is some truth to this: morality is usually food for flourishing. But to believe the two always go together is surely too optimistic. There are happy, fulfilled egotists and there are saints who sacrifice their own health, wealth or family lives for a higher good.

To focus too much on self-improvement is to risk directing our attention more towards the merely self-serving sense of betterment and to relegate the moral dimension to second place. To regain a proper focus, we could start by dropping the word 'self' and simply strive for improvement, in all its varieties. Coué's mantra should be changed to: 'Every day, in a significant way, I'll try to do better and better.'

This leads to the questions of what exactly it is we're trying to make better, and how far we should go. What people commonly believe they are trying to make the best of is their potential. Almost everyone thinks they know what their potential is, and many think they can spot it in others, even though by definition whether or not it really exists depends on the development of something that is not yet there. To say someone has the potential to be a great tennis player, for example, is to assume that they are not yet a great tennis player. So when we are thinking about as yet undeveloped abilities, turning potentiality into actuality usually involves a much higher degree of uncertainty than common talk of potential assumes.

For one thing, there are any number of reasons why we might simply fail to make real what is only possible. Resolve, emotional resources, or circumstances might fail us. Also, we might just be wrong. Many aspiring artists, for example, have at some stage to deal with the harsh truth that they are merely quite good and do not have what it takes to be truly exceptional. Potential that appears unlimited to youth may look more finite when seen through more experienced eyes.

Jean-Paul Sartre denounced potential for the false comfort it gives us through thoughts of what we could have been if things had been different. For him, a person is 'nothing else but the sum of his actions, nothing else but what his life is'. It's a false comfort to tell ourselves we could have done more, if circumstances had favoured us. Sartre insists that 'reality alone is reliable; that dreams, expectations and hopes serve to define a man only as deceptive dreams, abortive hopes, expectations unfulfilled'.[15] To dwell on potential is to define ourselves negatively, in terms of what we are not, rather than positively, for what we are. Potential left undeveloped is nothing more than a hypothetical ability that belongs in our dreams, not as a ghostly presence in our actual lives.

Gallic philosophers are not prone to understatement, and perhaps Sartre makes too much of this. But surely he is right to make us question the extent to which we too readily assume we know what we could be, or could have been. No one can see the future or alternative pasts. Potential that we are not actively trying to develop is nothing more than a hypothetical ability that we can never know we have.

So, it's good to strive for improvement, as long as we do so free from narcissism and illusions about what our potential might be. But then how far should we go? Despite the pitfalls of perfectionism, I think there is a sense in which it can sometimes be appropriate to strive towards impossible ideals. The thought behind this actually springs from its opposite, a principle attributed to Kant, that '*ought* implies *can*'.[16] In other words, it makes no sense to say that you should do something unless you are able to do so. You can't tell a pauper that he ought to give a million pounds to charity.

It sounds obvious, which is why I was struck when the philosopher Simon Critchley once told me that he thought that in ethics, ought implies *cannot*.[17] We should submit ourselves to a standard higher than we can ever achieve, because the moment that we become satisfied with our actions, we are lost. Something of this spirit is expressed in Jesus' injunction to love our neighbours as ourselves. The point is not that we can succeed. Rather, it is precisely because we can never claim to have raised ourselves high enough that we continue to strive to raise ourselves yet higher.

It's important to recognise that this is not the same as typical perfectionism. Unattainable aspirations only make sense when there is value in the increments on the way to them. If you want to be at a certain place at a certain time, for example, it's not half as good to get only halfway there – it's useless. If, on the other hand, you strive to be the best ukulele player in the country and you end up merely the best in town, that might be worth the effort. The perfectionist's problem is that second-best usually won't do, in which case she should either challenge this all-or-nothing assumption or make sure that her self-imposed ought is accompanied by a realistic can.

Second, striving for the impossible will drive you mad unless you remember that it is indeed impossible. Kid yourself that you can really do it and you are condemning yourself to a life of dissatisfaction. The problem with most perfectionists is not that they strive to be perfect, it's that they believe they can be.

THE PROBLEM WITH HAPPINESS

The Sage

—◦◦◦◦—

When psychology and philosophy filed for divorce about a hundred years ago, they faced the familiar dilemma of how to divide up the book collection. In the end, psychology left most volumes on happiness and the good life with philosophy, which dutifully left them to gather dust on the shelf. Now that psychology has returned to the subject with gusto, there is an urgent need to dig them out again.

One reason for this is that psychologists have tended to work with a thin conception of what happiness is, equating it with feeling good and measuring it by crude self-reporting surveys. But you only need to look at what people choose to do to see that they find all sorts of things deeply worthwhile that don't result in waves of positive emotion. The Austrian philosopher Ludwig Wittgenstein is a stark example of this. A troubled, intense figure, there is an entirely believable story that when he was struck down ill aged 62 and told he might have only a few days left to live, he replied, 'Good!' He did in fact die soon after, and his last reported words on his deathbed were: 'Tell them I've had a wonderful life.' His biographer, Ray Monk, did not find this surprising, whereas 'Tell them I've had a happy life' would have been completely baffling. 'Wittgenstein achieved a kind of purity of purpose that very few of us achieve', Monk once told me. 'A lot of the things that occupy my time, about my kids, about my mortgage, about day to day life, Wittgenstein successfully eliminated from his life, and that gives his life a kind of archetypal purity and concentration. There's something wonderful about that.'[18]

The standard way psychologists account for this kind of disconnect between the happy and the wonderful is to separate 'positive affect', which is the mood element of happiness, from life satisfaction, which is a person's assessment of how well their life is going. Even this is very hard to do. Martin Seligman, for instance, discovered that 70 per cent of a person's life satisfaction score depended on their mood at the time they reported it.[19]

In an attempt to go beyond this, Seligman has recently turned to the concept of flourishing. This is a good translation of *eudaimonia*, which Aristotle believed to be the highest goal of human life. Nevertheless, as a sign of how confused such discussions get, it is very often glossed simply as happiness, creating the false impression either that flourishing and happiness are basically the same thing, or that Aristotle advocated positive mood as our ultimate objective.

Aristotle was no dour miserabilist, and he accepted that pleasure was an important component of the good, flourishing life. But it was only one, and more important was living in accordance with our true natures as rational animals, using our heads and growing in wisdom. Sometimes this leads us to make choices that wipe the smiles from our faces but contribute to a sense of meaning or preserve our integrity. We value these things not primarily because they make us feel good (although they may do that too), but because we place a value on being a particular kind of person, living a particular kind of life.

Although psychology can help us understand this more clearly, it remains essentially a descriptive discipline that tries to give an accurate account of how people's minds actually work. The problem is that some more zealous practitioners and popularisers assume this can straightforwardly tell us what people *should* do. (See 'Psychology for philosophers' in Part Two.) For one thing, science deals with norms and averages, when we all have to struggle to live individual, particular lives. More fundamentally, science can tell us what degree of pleasure people get from things, for example, but it takes a philosophical analysis to decide whether we are taking pleasure in the right things and how much effort we should put into our own well-being anyway. There is surely something morally distasteful about devoting too much time to self-development when there are so many people in the world who are struggling simply to survive.

But perhaps the biggest risk of taking a scientific approach to *eudaimonia* is that the meaning and value of the things we do changes if we treat them as a means to an end. Take good relationships, for instance, a well-established indicator of well-being. The danger is that psychology can actually taint and devalue our relationships by making us think of others as routes to bliss rather than as people valued and loved for their own sake. For example, in *The Happiness Project*, Gretchen Rubin recounts an occasion on which she hugged her husband 'for at least six seconds – which, I happened to know from my research, is the minimum time necessary to promote the flow of oxytocin and serotonin, mood-boosting chemicals that promote bonding'.[20] Surely hugging with all this in mind is going to change the experience and turn something genuine and heartfelt into an instrumental technique.

Psychology certainly has a lot to teach us about what makes us happy. But as soon as we start thinking about what we should and should not do the issues become ethical, and we need to turn to philosophy – not to tell us what we should do, but to help us work it out for ourselves.

The Shrink

A handy tool in a therapist's toolbox, originally from Solution-Focused Brief Therapy, is the so-called 'miracle question', which goes something like this: 'Suppose that while you're asleep tonight a miracle happens and the problems that brought you here were solved. What would you notice in the morning? How would your life have changed? What would be different?' Too often the answer that comes back is: 'I'd just be happy.'

You, the therapist, try to press them, inquiring into what would be different if they were happy, what they would be doing, with whom, and so on. But sometimes people refuse to be pinned down, and happiness remains an evanescent rosy-tinted fantasy. This is the first problem with happiness: it's vague. There's little we can do to move towards it unless we manage to put some flesh on it.

But the pendulum has begun to swing in recent years. At one point, perhaps around the publication in 2005 of *Happiness*, the influential book by Richard Layard, the support for pursuing happiness seemed univocal. Even the Dalai Lama announced that the purpose of life was seeking happiness, which seems odd sitting next to the central Buddhist doctrine that life is suffering.[21] Then the dissenting voices got louder. Many in philosophy and psychology, including father of positive psychology Martin Seligman, took to denouncing happiness as a shallow main goal in life. Better to aim for well-being, or flourishing – richer, more nuanced and multi-dimensional concepts that make room for other things we may want for their own sake, like engagement with meaningful activities.[22]

To be sure, the pursuit of happiness does suffer from all kinds of contradictions. For a start, too much focus on it is self-defeating, since in practice the more we try to be happy the *less* happy we become. The harder you try to grasp it, the more happiness eludes you.

One reason for this is that we seem to be very poor at predicting what will in fact make us happy (or unhappy). As psychologist Dan Gilbert has argued, big changes in life circumstances, positive or negative, often make a surprisingly small and short-term difference to our happiness, before we revert to our customary levels of cheerfulness or gloom.[23]

Another reason might be that we often pin our hopes of being happy on some ideal scenario-to-come, when no major problems confront us and our situation is as satisfactory as can be wished. So even if, overcoming our vagueness, we manage to form some goals that we believe will get us to this enchanted realm, we might be too mesmerised by a hypothetical future to notice the happiness we can have now, in our imperfect present.

The hunt for happiness also risks raising the bar of our expectations far too much. Reading books and magazine articles on the topic, we could come to believe that happiness is our right and duty in life. But taking the attitude that we *must* ensure we're happy will make us vulnerable to disappointment, regret and self-blame when (not *if*) the world does not cooperate with our desires. We would do well to remember that happiness is hard to reach because 'the universe was not designed with the comfort of human beings in mind',[24] as psychologist Mihalyi Csikszentmihalyi has pointed out in *Flow*.

Does this mean we should ditch all attempts to be happy, or simply refine them? There are shades between having a gnawing devotion to the task and completely discarding it. As one of a number of things that contribute to a rich life, happiness does matter, and there is no reason why we shouldn't choose to do some things that make us happy simply because they do. And *doing* is the operative word here. According to psychologist Daniel Kahneman: 'The easiest way to increase happiness is to control your use of time. Can you find more time to do the things you enjoy doing?'[25]

If we start paying attention to what makes us happy and what gets in the way, we might notice patterns: some pleasures pass swiftly, or have painful consequences; others are longer-lasting and continue to make us happy long after they're over. We can learn from this and shift our energies towards things that provide fuller satisfaction, instead of getting distracted by those that have a strong but superficial attraction.

According to Viktor Frankl, psychiatrist and founder of *logotherapy*, what really matters is having a *reason* to be happy, and happiness will follow.[26] Whether or not it does follow, it seems like a good policy to direct our efforts to doing things we value and that give meaning to our life. This is perhaps the best way of understanding the familiar idea that happiness should be pursued 'indirectly'. Along similar lines, Bertrand Russell recommended that 'your interests be as wide as possible', which, among other things, would help to keep our own narrow concerns in perspective.[27]

But perhaps we also need to bring happiness down a notch or two. What we normally mean by happiness is after all just a feeling, or a mood, and moods and feelings are not entirely in our control. This is a good reason to avoid focusing on them too much. Both Morita Therapy and Acceptance and Commitment Therapy, for instance, regard as misguided our insistence on perpetuating positive feelings and escaping negative ones. It can't be done. Instead, we should let feelings come and go while we get on with what we value in life.

So rather than looking for the recipe for happiness, you could try to assemble the ingredients of a flourishing life, throwing into the mix: worthwhile activities that are important to you irrespective of feelings; goals that you believe will make you happier, so long as you keep them in perspective; paying closer attention to your own experience to discover what actually gives you fulfilment and delight in daily life, then making sure you spend time cultivating those things.

ON GOALS

The Shrink

At this very moment, people around the globe will be busy pursuing their goals. Losing weight is one of the most popular; other common ones are finding a life partner, improving one's work or financial situation, improving oneself. Being happy. Wherever you are, you don't have to look far to find advice on the correct way to set goals. Of course you know these should be SMART: specific, measurable, achievable, relevant and timed (or some version of this list). This seems unobjectionable. It's hardly worth disputing that, as a goal, something like 'I will go running for half an hour three times a week from next Monday' is superior to 'I will try to exercise more' – if indeed you wish to be fitter, are able to run, have a suitable place to do it and so on.

There is a little more room for discussion on how goals should be framed: is it better to adopt the goal of 'getting married', for instance, or that of 'joining a dating site'? In other words, should goals be expressed in terms of process or outcome? Many in the self-help business think we need both. It makes sense: the outcome goal of getting married is nicely complemented by the process goal of joining a dating site, or whatever else you may choose to do to reach it.

In our dogged pursuit of the results we desire we may be reluctant to admit that, useful though goal-setting is, it can be quite oppressive. We can become addicted to chasing goals. Our life can become so dominated by them that as soon as one is ticked off the list the next one pops up, before we even have time to congratulate ourselves. But this game is tiresome, full of fears of stalling, drifting, or being somehow left behind, and can't really be won. The thought of liberating ourselves from all this striving and just *being* for a while, with all our imperfections, seems at the same time delicious and mildly subversive. So should we ditch our goals and just go along with whatever life throws at us?

There is a sense in which we don't *have to* stretch ourselves, push ourselves out of our comfort zone, or do anything at all. But like all animals, we are purposeful creatures. Apathy is not a good state. A passive and static existence is not one that many would choose. It's good for us to be involved in activities that develop our capacities. A desire to improve ourselves and our circumstances is natural, admirable and to be taken seriously.

Psychiatrist Viktor Frankl, for instance, thought that the tension between what one is and what one should become was indispensable to mental well-being: 'What man actually needs is not a tensionless state but rather the striving and struggling for a worthwhile goal, a freely chosen task.'[28] Mihalyi Csikszentmihalyi similarly claims that: 'As long as it provides clear objectives, clear rules for action, and a way to concentrate and become involved, any goal can serve to give meaning to a person's life.'[29] In the flow theory that he originated, goals should be hard enough so they're not boring but not so hard as to create too much anxiety.

So some kind of forward movement seems important for human beings, and goals can be useful to focus the mind and direct our actions. But they don't have to be big leaps forward. It's possible to grow organically, without huge challenges, nudging ourselves here and there, continuing to learn, practising something a bit more difficult. Just keep moving.

To ensure we move in the right direction, it's advisable to do a little reflection on values before setting goals, since values create a more spacious environment for thinking about our life. The distinction between goals and values is explained in Acceptance and Commitment Therapy through the simile of a journey. Goals are like the sights you want to see on your journey, which you can tick off your list as you go along. Values on the other hand are like a compass showing the direction in which you want to travel, and in which you can continue to move as long as you wish.

So instead of focusing on a concrete goal like 'becoming a doctor', say, you could start with choosing a value to live by, such as 'helping people'. This has the advantage of helping us to stay close to what really matters, avoiding getting fixated on a particular goal, and creating flexibility, since there can be multiple ways of fulfilling the broader value. Even if training as a doctor became impossible, for whatever reason, there may be other relevant careers open to you.

Values should be probed somewhat. What values would you say are most important to you? Can you really own them? We need to check we haven't passively absorbed our values at some point without ever subjecting them to close scrutiny. It's also worth cross-checking them to see if one grossly contradicts another, as this can lead to conflicting goals. Unexamined values of commitment and freedom, for instance, can confuse our goals in the sphere of relationships.

Some honest reflection on our values can also help us to avoid the pitfall of giving up a goal as soon as the going gets tough. While we may want to, say, have a trim figure, other things being equal, we may not want it enough to make the required effort to diet and exercise (although that may change if our health comes to hinge on it, for instance). But if we have thought through our values we'll be more likely to set goals we are genuinely prepared to commit to.

There are other mistakes to avoid if we don't want to be slaves to goals. One is seriously underestimating the workings of chance in whether or not we reach the targets we have set ourselves. An excessive focus on outcome goals is especially treacherous, and leaves us hostages to fortune. If we believe it's entirely up to us to create the life we want, it will be difficult to be forgiving towards ourselves when we're thwarted. Another mistake is keeping our gaze so fixed over the horizon that we end up failing to appreciate what we have here and now. We should aim to balance striving and contentment, moving forward and noticing where we are. Goals are best married with going with the flow.

The Sage

The line between success and failure is not only thin, it's constantly moving. Take the British tennis player Tim Henman, for instance. The facts about his career are clear enough. He was the top-ranked British player for several years, won fifteen singles titles on the professional world tour and was at his peak ranked number four in the world. If that isn't a successful career, what is? However, Henman is remembered in tennis circles for being one of the best players in the history of the game never to have won a Grand Slam tournament: the international tour's most prestigious events. Indeed, he never even made it to a Grand Slam final. And so in interviews towards the end of his career, he repeatedly had to address 'this perception that I'm a failure'.[30]

If you want to understand the meaning and importance of goals and their achievement, Henman's career is a good place to start. Most obviously, his experience shows how relative notions of success are. 'I've been rated this year as the fourth best player on the planet', he told an interviewer in 2005. 'If that's your idea of failure, then fine.' In many ways it's perfectly right that how we set and measure goals and expectations varies with circumstances. Better and worse can only be measured from the position we find ourselves in. What is pernicious is the belief that you must always achieve more than you have already done.

If reaching goals should not be an imperative, nor should it be an expectation. Two people may be equally committed to doing all they can to achieve something, but one might merely hope that they will succeed, while the other blindly believes that they will. To live in hope without expectation is more honest and makes us more prepared to confront setbacks or even ultimate failure.

Of course, there are some who argue that you need the conviction that you will succeed in order to do so. They fear that any dilution of this, any acceptance of the possibility of failure, will open up a chink of doubt which will corrode determination and application. If this is true of some or most of us, it may be another regrettable symptom of our inability to deal with too much reality, and we may have to choose between taking the more truthful or the most effective path. But if it is indeed sometimes true, perhaps it's because we have made it true. Our belief that self-belief has to be absolute means that we inevitably see any self-doubt as a sign of weakness to be expunged.

In other words, self-doubt undermines will only because we have not learned to live with doubt.

There is, however, a more fundamental question about what goals are worth pursuing in the first place. There is a tendency to shy away from this question, as it requires us to judge how worthwhile different activities are, and one of the new commandments of our times is 'Thou Shalt Not Judge Others'. But in extreme cases at least, we all accept that some goals are so wrong they should not be pursued at all, such as 'purifying' the genetic stock of the population, or preventing people from holding religious beliefs. In many other cases, although we might not judge a goal to be morally wrong, we can't help but think it's misguided. I mean, if success means getting into the *Guinness Book of Records* for having the world's largest collection of airline sick bags (5,568 and counting) as it did for Niek Vermeulen of the Netherlands, is it really worth having?

Trying to explain exactly what's wrong with adopting such goals, however, is extremely difficult. The most obvious suggestion is that such goals are too trivial and ephemeral: you get your moment of triumph and entry in the record book, and that's it. But the problem is that most things look trivial if we look at them the wrong (or perhaps right) way, and everything is ephemeral. It's vanity, for instance, to think that having a best-selling book or winning a literary prize is not ephemeral. Given the fickleness of taste and the caprice of fashion and literary critics, it would also be wrong to take any such success as a reliable indicator of importance.

If we think worthwhile goals have to be both important and enduring, then it's time to despair.

So here's another suggestion. The best goals are ones that focus on *doing* and *being*, not on *having done*. Whenever a goal is to have done something, whether it's to have won a Grand Slam or eaten more baked beans in one minute than any other human in recorded history, then the problem is that achieving the goal leaves you with nothing left to do, unless you adopt yet another goal, and keep the cycle going until you tire of life or it tires of you. If, however, your goal is to be a good cook, for example, to do good cooking, then achieving that goal means you have succeeded in living a form of life that has more meaning and satisfaction to you, a life that is filled with more of what you value.

It's important to notice that adopting this kind of goal sometimes involves focusing on having done certain things too. If you try to be the best tennis player you can, for instance, then you will hope to have won some tournaments by the time you retire. If you want to be a writer, then you will certainly want to have finished writing something eventually. The critical point is that each of these goals has its value because pursuing it requires you to do and be what you want to do and be. That is what gives it deep worth, not simply the fact that you have done them and so added to your list of achievements.

Another way in which being and doing may relate to having done is when a goal is altruistic. For example, providing clean water to dozens of villages in Africa is surely as worthwhile a goal as you can imagine. The reason is that, if you succeed, you will have changed for the better how people live, enabling them to pursue what they want to be and do.

Still, it would be a fudge to avoid saying anything at all about what sorts of ways of doing and being count as real achievement and which don't. When philosophers have suggested answers to this, however, the suspicion is that their pronouncements are conveniently self-serving. Aristotle, for instance, thought the right way to live was 'in accordance with reason, or at least not entirely lacking it',[31] which sounds a little too like a baker preaching the indispensability of bread.

And yet surely there is something to this. For Aristotle it was important that we should live in such a way that makes the most of our distinctive human capacities, not just to live as animals or 'mere' humans. Life in accordance with reason is, he wrote, 'divine compared with human life' and we ought to 'do all we can to live in accordance with the highest element within us, for even if its bulk is small, in its power and value it far exceeds everything'.[32] Maybe he did not consider seriously enough the possibility that the best part of us, the spark of the divine, might involve things other than just reason. Humans are not only distinguished by their ability to reason, but by the capacities to shape wood, dance, make music, love with understanding, cultivate crops and so on. If we make it our goal to live doing these things and we succeed, we surely will have achieved something worthwhile, even if we have not reached the pinnacle of human potential.

BEING TRUE TO YOURSELF

STANLEY WAS DEEPLY DISAPPOINTED WHEN, HIGH IN THE TIBETAN MOUNTAINS, HE FINALLY FOUND HIS TRUE SELF.

The Shrink

There you are – you try therapy, meditation, travel and adventure, in the hope of 'finding yourself', and all the time your real self was the one you left behind at the office.

Jokes apart, the game of discovering the real self behind the mask is widespread both in therapy and in life. Unearthing this hidden inner self is something that people seem to desire deeply. Mysterious distinctions appear in the process: this person is authentic, that one inauthentic, this way of being is real, that one not real. Now, it's easy to understand what we mean by an authentic Picasso. But an authentic self?

If we get caught up in this game we can end up utterly confused, trying to work out whether we or others are being 'real' and 'authentic', or 'putting on a mask'. In some circles, for instance, you would be considered inauthentic if you dealt with life events through humour, since you would be distancing yourself from your feelings. That makes sense only if 'being real' has been narrowly defined as showing emotion, spontaneity and vulnerability.

But isn't all of you real? Let's say someone is not in the habit of even registering their emotions, let alone displaying them to others. Perhaps there is some specific sense in which that can be said to be 'not real'. But in another way that person is being perfectly 'real'. There may or may not be seething emotion 'under the surface', but even if there is, it's surely the whole package – the emotions *and* the stiff upper lip – that makes up that complex individual.

In practice, the question of whether someone is being 'real' is not that interesting or productive. There are better ones: whether they are being honest, with themselves and others; which patterns of thought and behaviour work for them and which don't; whether their actions are in line with their values, with their vision of who they want to be; what the costs are of maintaining certain ways of being.

The idea of a true self, of some kind of essential core we must be faithful to, comes into play in all sorts of daily situations like jobs, or relationships: should you grit your teeth and persevere with a job that 'isn't you'? How far should you go against the grain of your personality in order to meet someone else's needs?

This kind of thinking is reinforced in books and magazine articles on personality types. We may have moved on from sanguine, choleric, melancholic and phlegmatic types. But we have many others. Only some of the most popular are: introvert and extravert; sensing, feeling, thinking, intuitive; type A and type B. Especially in favour at the moment, though, are the Big Five: open, conscientious, extravert, agreeable, neurotic.

Then there are labels of identity, which we use to fix notions of ourselves. You might be British, a parent, a teacher, amateur photographer, squash player. Or a retired business person, a keen gardener. Or whatever. It's useful to capture our identity in a handful of shiny labels that we can show to the world. 'Look, this is who I am', we say.

It's also reassuring. Being able to describe ourselves with a string of sturdy nouns creates an illusion of solidity, soothing the existential insecurities that lurk behind most façades. It fosters a sense of belonging, binding us to people in the same group. Perhaps surprisingly, this comforting effect can surface even when a label points to something negative – seeing yourself as a victim of the economic downturn, for instance, at least puts you in the company of others.

But while our self-descriptions are convenient short-hands, they can become rigid. Too strong a sense of identity can lead to being inflexible and unwilling to compromise. You might say: 'This is what I'm like', or 'That's not me'. Holding on too tightly to particular identity markers means we can be left with an unfillable hole at the centre of our existence if they are taken away. Feeling bereft of identity is a common experience for many people who retire after spending a lifetime married to their job, for instance, and of course even more common for mothers whose children have left home.

Making the edges of who we are too sharp can also undermine flexibility. You may end up avoiding activities and situations that you perceive as 'not you', missing out on things that could expand your identity. When we use broad-stroke descriptions to draw attention to salient aspects of ourselves we would do well to remember that what is salient can change, and we also contain shifting, unlabelled potentialities that may yet come to the fore. The inclinations and dispositions we show from early on in life are not infinitely plastic, but nor are they rigidly fixed.

Aristotle believed that the ability to change is what distinguishes human beings from other entities in nature, which can only obey the laws of physics. He thought we could develop a virtuous character by changing our habits, and that this was something for which we had to take personal responsibility. People are 'responsible for being unjust by doing wrong, or intemperate by spending their time in drinking and the like; in each sphere people's activities give them the corresponding character'.[33]

It's natural, even inevitable, to come to think of our habits as 'who we are', and trying to counter them can seem just 'not us'. But this may simply be our old habits putting up a fight. Since habits rest mainly on performing established, automated sequences of behaviour in a usual environment, they can be changed by disrupting one or the other. For instance, research by psychologist David Neal has found that eating habits can be altered by switching to the non-dominant hand.[34] Establishing completely new habits, on the other hand, relies more on specific and detailed planning of where, when and how the new behaviours are to occur. So we are not stuck with what we've got. Even if changing habits feels uncomfortable and alien, it's worth persevering.

But an excessive belief in our own flexibility can lead us to persist with behaviours that we can sustain only at a cost. Take Ivan and Rebecca. He is undemonstrative and she expressive. (It could be any other clash – tidy and untidy, or high and low sex drive.) He considers this a fixed trait of his, she believes she can choose to be different. The mismatch if these two get together can be damaging, as Rebecca bends over backwards to mould herself to Ivan's unemotional shape to the point of doing without the affection she deeply values in a relationship. The self-transformation she's trying to perform just doesn't fit in with who she is and wants to be, but she doesn't realise it until she has gone through a lot of heartache.

Our attitudes in this sphere are not always consistent, however, and we often oscillate between wanting to be faithful to our self and believing in our transformational powers. Unfortunately we don't really know what we are capable of until we try, and we often both over- and under-estimate our potential to change ourselves. Our challenge is to work out the limits of our own malleability and sort the situations in which it is important to stretch ourselves from those in which we should instead go with the grain. If you are of a shy and introverted disposition, for instance, it may take considerable effort to push yourself to be a polit-ician, or work in PR. You have to decide whether the effort is well spent, or the price worth paying.

That's easier said than done. Where can we find guid-ance? Our 'inner self' may or may not deliver a pronounce-ment. It's more reliable to reflect honestly on what is possible, what the costs are, on our deeply held values and our cherished notions of what kind of person we want to be. You can call this being true to yourself, if you like.

The Sage

The trouble with the idea of being true to yourself is that it assumes we know what we are being true to. In fact, the nature of the self is somewhat elusive, and the best description neuroscience and philosophy can give of it flies in the face of common sense.

Theories of self divide into two broad categories.[35] On the 'pearl' view, there is something permanent and unchanging at the heart of each of us, and that is what makes us who we are. This seems to be how we intuitively think of ourselves, but if you try to identify what this pearl is, most serious thinkers about the self agree you can't find it. Almost all philosophers and even many theologians agree that there is no such thing as an immaterial soul, a non-physical core of you that can survive the death of your body. Neuroscientists are as close to unanimity as is humanly possible in thinking that sense of self is not the function of one part of the brain, a spot where all experience comes together.

The alternative view is that we are not pearls, but 'bundles'. You are the sum of your thoughts, feelings, experiences, desires, memories and so on; you are not a separate *thing* that *has* them. This may sound weird, but it only makes us like everything else in the universe. Water, for example, just is the organised sum of two hydrogen and one oxygen atoms: it's not a separate thing that has these three atoms attached to it. In the same way, we are just organised collections of thoughts, feelings, sensations, memories and so on, not discrete things that have them.

Why then do we fall for the pearl illusion? Because this bundle is kept very tightly bound by what several neuroscientists call the 'autobiographical self'. Experiments can reveal the extent to which experience at any given moment turns out to be far less unified than we commonly suppose. It's as though different parts of the brain are aware of different things, not always consciously sharing information. But almost straight away, some of these experiences are committed to memory, and it's in that process that they are made to form a more coherent, seamless narrative in which we have one centre of consciousness, one life history.

Does it make a difference if we try to see ourselves more as dynamic, changing bundles and try to counter the intuition that we are fixed, abiding pearls? I think it can. If we have no permanent, unchanging core, then it follows that who we are is not just a given. Rather, we become who we are in part through our actions and choices. Being you is an exercise in constant self-creation, although it's vital to realise that this is not *ex nihilo*. We are fashioned not just by our own thoughts and actions, but by our bodies, our societies and our past experiences. Real life is not a clockwork mechanism but a fluid, complex, dynamic system. As parts of this system it doesn't help to think of ourselves as absolute slaves or masters of it. Nothing is completely fixed or free because everything is affected by what surrounds it. We should simply change what we can, being aware that we cannot control everything.

Think of how this would apply to character. If we think of this as being something fixed by nature, nurture or both, we risk stripping away all sense of responsibility. If the good and bad are just made that way, what's the point of praise or blame? If, on the other hand, we think of character as something we can in part shape for ourselves, then we can see how, by cultivating good character, we have a real effect on the quality of our future choices and relationships.

This is even more important if you distinguish 'character' from 'personality'. Whereas we tend to think of personality non-judgementally, as a set of reasonably settled traits, character often has a moral dimension. We talk of someone being of good or bad, upright or depraved character. So even if you think personality is relatively fixed, there is no reason to think that moral character must also be so. An impulsive person may be more vulnerable to crimes of passion, for example, but that doesn't mean he has no control over his actions.

Ideas of fixed cores also infect the ways in which we apply labels of identity: ethnic, religious, national, political. People say they don't like to be pigeon-holed, but what they really appear to mean is that they don't want others to do the labelling for them. Left to our own devices, we happily categorise ourselves in any number of ways, probably because our identities give us a feeling of belonging, and this in turn gives us a stronger sense of who we are and our place in the world.

Identities therefore point to both what makes us uniquely different from others and what makes us the same. It seems we desire both to be *a part of* and *apart from* the wider mass of society. And so it should be. You cannot understand what it means to be a human individual unless you understand the extent to which we inhabit both a shared social world and private subjective reality. Labels of identity help us to make sense of this dual nature. Each identity we take on is shared with others, but together they form a set which, if not quite unique, is at least highly personalised.

But because labels of identity can refer only to what we have in common with others, they can never capture our uniqueness. Our multiple identities are like an incomplete list of ingredients that fails to specify how much to use of each, or even how they should be combined. That's one reason why it's such a grave error to bring identities too far into politics. The moment we start to think of, say, 'the Jewish community' or 'road users' as a homogeneous group, sharing some core element of identity, we end up crudely lumping together people who may have only one thing in common.

Excessively firm ideas of character, personality and group identity are just three ways in which we can come to think of our 'true selves' as being more constant, predictable, knowable and fixed than they really are. This challenges received opinion about integrity, which sees it as requiring constancy, standing firm and refusing to change. But if we are indeed much more dynamic and fluid than the pearl view implies, then perhaps we are more true to ourselves when we accept our contradictions, fluctuations and evolution over time. The person who remains the same from one decade to the next is thus not being true to herself, but true to a false idea of self.

WHAT SHOULD YOU DO
BEFORE YOU DIE?

The Shrink

⟶ ❧ ⟵

On the wall of a retreat centre I used to go to, there was a sign saying: 'Things to do today: breathe in, breathe out.' Inspiring or confusing? It's certainly refreshing: the pressure to do, achieve, accumulate, is all around and hard to escape.

If you're fortunate enough to have the income and opportunity, you might feel that life is a bit like a dazzling toy shop sometimes. With all the places to see, books to read, music to hear, you need never be bored. But the choice can be bewildering, despite the assistance of websites directing you to the best mountains to climb, exotic sunsets to admire, wild animals to photograph before you die, even helping you to tick them off like items on a shopping list.

Engaging in new experiences is undoubtedly a good thing. Instead of going through your days trundling along habitual rails, you can choose to do things that stretch and challenge you. You can open your mind to the unfamiliar. Putting yourself in slightly unpredictable situations brings you face to face with yourself, testing but also expanding your flexibility. In effect, you get more out of life.

And aren't we told that keeping mentally and physically active, pushing ourselves to learn new things, can help us to age better and even keep diseases like Alzheimer's at bay? Then there is the research telling us that experiences have a much greater impact on people's happiness than acquiring new objects.

But we shouldn't assume that doing ever more is the only way to spend our time well. For a start, if you rely on novelty to keep life interesting you could end up on a perpetual treadmill, always seeking the next thrill. You could fall prey to a sense of inadequacy if for whatever reason you fail to keep up. Like everything else, diversity of experience will become oppressive if taken as a 'must', even if you're the kind of person who thrives on it.

Introducing a note of scepticism in the otherwise deserved praise of new experiences doesn't imply it's OK to squander our life doing nothing but watching television, or drinking ourselves into a stupor, making no effort to learn anything or cultivate meaningful relationships. Our time on earth is limited, and the saddest thing we can do is waste it. What we need to ask ourselves is what 'wasting' really means for us.

While a certain amount of novelty can certainly be valuable, there are other ways of switching off the autopilot. In *Flow*, Mihalyi Csikszentmihalyi tells the story of Serafina, an elderly peasant living in a hamlet in the Italian Alps, whose life had always revolved around milking the cows, taking them to the pasture, tending the orchard, cutting hay, carding wool. A hard life, but one utterly intertwined with landscape, people, animals. If she could have whatever she wanted, that is exactly what she would choose to do. Does such a life really lack challenge and excitement?

Whether we are wasting time or not depends to a large extent on how we relate to the world around us. The excitement of new experiences is not the only good in life. There are other things that are just as valuable – simplicity, contentment, savouring the small pleasures and textures of daily life. We can restore sparkle to our routine by doing things more mindfully.

The rhythm of the seasons is a good example of something that appears the same year after year but will amply reward paying more attention. True, we will notice the same sorts of things punctuating the passing of the months: the blackbirds will start singing on roofs and trees towards the end of February, the summer will bring poppies and honeysuckle, and berries of all kinds will indicate that autumn is on its way. But the more we pay attention the more we see, and the more unique each day will be.

We can't always say from the outside whether precious time is being wasted. An outwardly conventional existence can brim with appreciation of the big and small things that make life worthwhile. An adventurous one can be devoid of it. A rich life can be one in which a few things have been experienced deeply.

Montaigne says we are fools to think that days without achievement have been idle or wasted. 'What! Have you not lived?' he writes. 'That is not only the fundamental, but the most noble of your occupations. … Have you been able to reflect on your life and control it? Then you have performed the greatest work of all. … Our great and glorious masterpiece is to live properly. All other things – to reign, to lay up treasure, to build – are at the best but little aids and additions.'[36]

How many new experiences we engage in, of what kind and how often, should depend on our personality, values and circumstances. But whatever else we do, we would be strongly advised to keep learning, savour every day, be mindful. Bungee jumping is optional.

The Sage

The race to do as much as possible before we reach our expiry date is rooted in a justifiable desire to experience life in its fullest intensity, squeezing out as much from each second as is possible. However, as the Danish existentialist Søren Kierkegaard acutely observed, the end result is often a life that is empty, not full. It becomes like trying to fill a sieve from a fountain of champagne. The present moment always eludes us: the moment we try to grasp it, it has already become the past.

The problem is that there is a real sense in which we are

trapped in what Kierkegaard called the 'aesthetic' sphere of existence.[37] Life is a present tense phenomenon: we can recall the past and anticipate the future but can only *be* in the here and now. But that truth is only half the story. In another sense, we do indeed exist *over time* as well as *at a time*, through our memories, intentions and projects. Life in this 'ethical' sphere requires us to attend to more than just the thrills of the moment. As any hangover reminds us, living only for today can cause a headache for tomorrow.

Kierkegaard recognised that the aesthetic and ethical realms are both real and that no life is fully human if it doesn't embrace both. However, he believed there was no rational way of reconciling the two. The only way forward was to embrace the contradiction and take a leap of faith into the religious sphere, which for him meant the central paradox of Christianity: God made man, the infinite made finite. The aesthetic and ethical can be brought together only by the sacrifice of reason.

I think Kierkegaard's diagnosis was spot-on, but his prescription rash. For a better way forward, one that points to what we really should prioritise before we die, we can look to a more modern, scientific take on Kierkegaard's spheres. Nobel laureate psychologist Daniel Kahneman has come up with a way of understanding the human mind that has an uncanny similarity to the one devised by the Danish armchair psychologist over a century earlier. On the basis of much experimental evidence, Kahneman distinguishes between two 'selves' we each have within us. One is the experiencing self, the self that exists only in the moment. It usually works intuitively, automatically, unconsciously. The other is the remembering self, the reflective, rational part that muses on what the experiencing self has done and will do, and that ties together the fragmented moments of experiencing into a coherent-seeming autobiographical narrative.[38]

The most striking experiment that shows the difference between the two was done on patients who had to endure a painful colonoscopy. The counterintuitive finding from this was that it's possible to get patients to perceive the experience as less traumatic and painful by causing them *more* pain. Here's how it works. As the procedure is taking place, you get them to rate how much pain they are in, on a scale of one to ten, at regular short intervals. After the procedure is finished, you get them to rate how painful it was as a whole. If the remembering self perceives pain as the experiencing self feels it, the latter score should just track the former: the more pain reported at the time, the more painful the overall experience would be judged. But this isn't how it works. Most importantly, the remembering self attaches much more importance to how the experience ends than how it started or went in the middle. So, if the last phase of the procedure is very painful, the remembering self rates the experience as a whole to be much worse and is also less inclined to repeat the procedure in future. But if the experience in a second case is exactly the same, with the only difference being the addition of some lower-level pain after this intense discomfort, the remembering self rates the experience as a whole more favourably, and is more willing to put up with the intrusion again. The extra, mild discomfort makes the pain that preceded it less traumatic to remember, because it's now part of a narrative that ends more happily.[39]

The question Kahneman's work raises is: Which self should we put first? They are not literally two selves, so we cannot ask which is the real you. But we can ask which part matters more to you. The answer surely has to be the remembering self, since that is the reflective part that actually judges what matters, while the experiencing self just feels good, bad or indifferent. After all, it's the remembering self that asks questions like 'What should I do before I die?' in the first place. Only the remembering self is aware of a life narrative in which it matters what has come before the last two words: The End.

This to me provides the key to unlocking Kierkegaard's conundrum. The remembering self inhabits the ethical sphere. But this self has no content other than that which is provided by the experiencing self. The moments of life provide the raw materials from which the life story is constructed, so it's important that we try to make our experiences count. What's vital to realise, however, is that this construction is not a simple additive process. Ten pleasant moments might pass and vanish from our memory, while one unpleasant one might end up becoming a pivotal episode. Even the most intense moment of pleasure takes on a different value, depending on where in a life story it comes. The enjoyment of a great meal, for instance, is not just a function of chemicals in the food interacting with taste buds. It can make a big difference, even to how flavours are sensed, when, where and with whom the meal is savoured. More importantly still, unpleasant experiences might form more meaningful chapters than empty but pleasurable ones.

So when thinking about what to do before you die, you need to think not of accumulating positive experiences, but of doing the kinds of things that will contribute to a more satisfying life story. This is missed by the person who heeds the modern imperative to do as much as possible before she dies and so becomes the Kierkegaardian aesthete *par excellence*. She may know that every moment has immense value, but she doesn't know how to value it. It's certainly true that we need to make the most of the short, fleeting life we have. However, to do that requires planning our journey along the passage of time carefully, not just making as many stops at the most superficially fun places along the way as possible.

BEING TORN

The Sage

❦

Like children offered ice cream or cake, we often respond
to demands of 'either/or' with the thought, why not 'both/
and'? At the root of much ambivalence is a failure to accept
the disappointing truth that both/and just isn't possible,
because many of life's most fundamental values just don't
fit together. Consider, for instance, independence and interdependence. We consider it a good thing that we are able
to think and fend for ourselves, that we are not just sheep
in a crowd. At the same time, we appreciate that there are
benefits of belonging to families and communities that are
open to us only if we are prepared to give up some independence. But you cannot have perfect independence and
interdependence: to have more of one is to have less of the
other. And what might be a good trade-off for one person
at one time may look like a bad deal for another – or even
the same – person at another time.

Many other important values are plural in the same
way. We value breadth of knowledge, but also depth, and
the wider you spread yourself, the shallower you are able to
delve into anything. One of the most common experiences
of pluralism is the pull towards both a high-achieving
career and a full family life, and a refusal to accept that

there are bound to be trade-offs if you want both leads to all sorts of problems and self-deceptions.

If values are indeed plural in this way, then unless we can decide once and for all which of the competing ones really matters the most, we are bound to end up in situations where we resolve to pursue one and are then deflected by the appeal of the other. And the point of pluralism is that we can't construct a neat hierarchy of these values either. They are, in the jargon, incommensurable: they cannot be measured against a single, shared standard. There just is no objective answer as to which matters most. It would be like trying to say whether Stilton is a better cheese than Fermat was a mathematician. Even if we reject pluralism and say that there is a single scale against which we can rank all values, it would be asking too much of people to do this when not even philosophers can agree on how they should be arranged.

I think that the lens of pluralism often explains ambivalent behaviour better than other standard psychological explanations, such as weakness of will or fear of failure. True, if I look back at times when I have persevered too much with something that in some sense I knew wasn't right, fear of failure may well have had something to do with it. But as an explanation for why people don't leave bad marriages, abandon failing businesses before debts get too high, or stay in a soul-destroying but high-status job, I don't think it goes deep enough. Often it isn't fear of failure as such that's the issue, but a sense in which an outcome appears to contradict deeply held values. You stick with that relationship because you want to be the kind of faithful, loving person who doesn't abandon your partner as soon as the going gets tough. You don't give up on your business because running it has been your dream and you'd love nothing more than to be able to continue doing so. You stay in the job because you value the challenge, or maybe just the status and money, if you're honest.

Rather than the key being a negative – fear of failure – too much persistence can be the result of a positive: an attachment to the value of the thing you persevere with. The mistake is simply to allow this value to override all others, to believe that giving up means renouncing it, rather than simply balancing it.

Although it can be impossible or destructive to maintain ambivalent behaviour, pluralism suggests it can be healthy to maintain ambivalent attitudes and beliefs. We may have to give up some freedom to enjoy the rewards of an interdependent relationship, for instance, but we can do so without pretending to ourselves and others that there are no real benefits to the independence we have relinquished.

Pluralism, however, does not mean that every value is worth holding. Sometimes, if we are ambivalent, we really should give up one of the competing desires or values. One problem with self-help – and even many forms of therapy – is that it usually treats a person's desires as givens, not to be challenged. Whatever a person wants – to lose weight, to feel less anxious, to save a relationship – is taken to be a valid end, and efforts are then concentrated on the means of achieving it. Heaven forfend the suggestion that the destination isn't worth the journey.

I suspect that a failure to consider just this possibility lies behind a large amount or unresolved ambivalence. In the absence of any truly deep thought about what really would make life better, we just leap on one of any number of things that our culture values and rewards, even if they are in deep tension. We aspire to eat more healthily but also more extravagantly; we want to develop our 'spiritual side' but we also want one of those lovely new tablet devices; we want to make progress professionally, but we also want to spend more time with our families. All of these are things that may indeed be worthwhile, but unless we know why they matter to us personally, we will find ourselves repeatedly torn, as the pursuit of one takes us further from another.

Making a decision requires accepting that we simply can't do everything, and that following one path inevitably leaves others untrodden. So we can be stuck at the crossroads, decided to go one way but unable to shake off the worry that the road not taken might be better. You can't delay your journey indefinitely, until you are certain your choice is perfect. But it doesn't have to be perfect, only good enough. And if it turns out not even to be that, you'll just have to change direction later.

Ambivalence is therefore avoidable to the extent that we can recognise the need to make either/or choices and act accordingly, but also inevitable because different options have different attractions, and which seems better will not necessarily be the same at all moments. To experience ambivalence is not to deal with an aberration, but a permanent fact of life that we often do a good job of conveniently ignoring.

The Shrink

Let's start from the beginning, from what David Eagleman refers to as the 'representative democracy' of our mind: 'There is an ongoing conversation among the different factions in your brain, each competing to control the single output channel of your behavior. As a result, you can accomplish the strange feats of arguing with yourself, cursing at yourself, and cajoling yourself to do something.'[40]

1. So you're conflicted. Out of your internal multitudes, a faction wants to continue to be in a stable relationship with your long-term partner, another doesn't want to give up the excitement of an affair.

Congratulations. You're a normal human being. It's very common for us humans to feel one way and another about things, changing our minds, surfing multiple waves of all sorts of contradictory desires. Many things are in competition when we are considering what to do, which reasons and values to pursue and which to let go of. But a lot of it boils down to short-term gratification vs. long-term benefit.

We can't always have it all, so we need to jump one way or another. Often things resolve themselves in their own time in between reflecting and reacting to life situations. Before too long the agony ends and a decision emerges that sticks.

2. But sometimes – too often – we get stuck in the ambivalence. Then we keep bouncing from one side to the other like a ball. We postpone the decision. We are wildly inconsistent, acting sometimes on one thing sometimes the other. Then it seems like we've made a decision, but it means little. We still feel pulled the other way. We 'unmake' the decision. And so on.

So you're uncomfortable about it and keep thinking you must put a stop to it, but in the meantime you continue your affair.

3. So far, all you have made is a mere decision. Things start getting more interesting if we introduce a more exotic version: the *all-things-considered judgement*. Of course it's not possible to consider *all* factors. But it *is* possible to reflect honestly on all the factors you can think of, critically examining them and rating them in order of importance.

An all-things-considered judgement factors in all the benefits and costs, short-term and long-term, including how hard your proposed undertaking is likely to be and how much effort it will take. It's the decision you arrive at after you've taken all of that into account.

So you get out your notebook or your laptop and make a list of pros and cons. On the one hand you value the stability, affection and support that your relationship gives you, plus you don't want to risk hurting people around you. On the other, it seems intolerable to miss out on the excitement of the affair, which makes you feel young and alive, in fact what life is all about.

4. That exercise may or may not lead to a considered decision. Sometimes no matter how hard you probe your pros and cons no overwhelming winner emerges: perhaps the values are too finely balanced, perhaps there are too many unknowns. Then any decision you make is fragile, and you're always poised to slip back into the paralysis of ambivalence.

5. Let's say there is a clear winner. Great, but even that doesn't eliminate the motivational split, the fact that you still feel a pull in the opposite direction. Unfortunately our desires, motivations, inclinations don't always line up with our all-things-considered judgements.

So you can see clearly, in black and white in front of you, that the affair doesn't make sense. Your relationship is really important to you and it would be really foolish to risk losing it, and hurting people, for the sake of a thrill.

Perhaps there are other things you can do to feel alive. But still …

(Of course you could have found the opposite: you could instead see clearly that you and your partner have grown apart, that your relationship has become cursory and based only on habit and that you need to find the courage to move on. But still …)

6. That's when weakness of will can happen. (Also see 'Will and resolution'.) Despite a sound all-things-considered judgement, we end up doing the opposite, and acting on reasons that we ourselves had considered secondary.

According to Aristotle, we are weak-willed (or lacking in self-control) when we act against our own judgement about what course of action we should follow. We behave as if that knowledge were temporarily lost to us – as if we were 'asleep, mad or drunk'.[41]

So there you are: you're completely clear that all things considered you should end your affair, but instead you pick up the phone and arrange another meeting.

7. But wait a minute: was the decision right in the first place? Or had you made a mistake in your calculations when you did your list of pros and cons? This question is well worth asking. But it could equally be the voice of self-deception. Remember that despite reaching a considered judgement you're still pulled in the other direction, so at times of temptation you'll naturally doubt your conclusion.

The part of you that wants to have excitement and feel alive, for instance, could be trying to avoid having its particular brand of gratification squashed. So you end up wondering whether you were wrong, whether you should have given more weight to this need.

How can you tell whether you should reconsider your decision or simply expose the self-deception for what it is? Go back to your list of pros and cons when you're away from temptation. Do you reach the same conclusion about what you should do? And if you act against it, do you tend to regret it? If the answer is yes, then there's probably nothing wrong with the decision. It's just that a part of you that desires something different is refusing to accept your verdict and trying to assert its authority. It's what Eagleman calls the 'I-want-it-now system' putting up a fight.

8. If your judgement *was* right, you need to learn to resist temptation. But what does that mean? It doesn't mean just promising yourself that next time you'll do better. When you get near the temptation, you won't. It does mean making some kind of commitment to stop yourself acting on your future shifts in motivation. It means identifying the situations in which you're most likely to backslide, looking ahead and acquiring the tools to deal with them.

In the case of your affair, putting yourself in a tempting situation may mean frequenting places where you are likely to run into your lover, for instance.

9. Aristotle thought that lack of self-control happens through either impetuosity or weakness. To update the terminology, it seems to me that there are two main mechanisms: impulsive action (acting before you have the time to reflect) and self-deception (you convince yourself that 'This time it's OK because ...').

So for instance you send an email to your lover without thinking. Or convince yourself that you're incapable of ending the affair, or that you'll see your lover one more time, or that you can continue to see your lover as a friend, and so on.

10. There are many strategies you can use to counter those mechanisms. You could avoid the places of temptation. You could get a friend to remind you of your decision. You could carry your list of pros and cons around and look at it frequently. You could learn to observe your urges. It could be useful to acquaint yourself with your particular rationalisations and write them down, together with why they're false.

Let's go back to Eagleman's representative democracy of our mind, the 'ongoing conversation among the different factions in your brain'. Your job is to manage the disagreements and implement consensus decisions – to do what you can, among the shouting and insurrection, to bring this house to order.

DEALING WITH EMOTIONS

The Sage

—◦◦◦◦—

The head and the heart have often been portrayed as two organs in constant battle. In Plato's dialogue *Phaedrus*, intellect is a charioteer, pulled by one horse of noble passion while trying to whip his unruly companion into line.[42] David Hume would have thought the charioteer a self-deluded fool, for in reality it's the horses who are deciding on the chariot's direction: 'reason is and ought only to be the slave of passions.'[43]

There is some truth in both models. But where they mislead is in suggesting that the head and heart work against each other. In fact, unless they worked in tandem, both would be unrecognisable. Often, if not always, we would not feel the way we do unless we thought the way we do. We desire things that we believe will give us pleasure, for instance, and if we find out they don't, our lust soon subsides. Similarly, anger is calmed if we come to believe that someone has not done us an injustice after all. Rather than a charioteer, perhaps Plato should have conjured up images of a horse-whisperer, who calms an agitated stallion by reasoning with it, not beating it.

Hume comes closest to the truth, however, in recognising that the head needs the heart even more than the heart needs the head, since there is nothing in pure rationality that can provide us with any motivation. Nor can moral reasoning get off the ground without an empathetic understanding of the welfare of others. Without any input from emotion or feeling, reason is merely a cold, mechanical method of calculation. It can help us work out what the consequences of our actions might be, but it cannot tell us whether they are desirable.

On the other hand, reason is vital for keeping an eye on the unreliable testimony of automatic emotional responses. For example, philosophers since antiquity have been warning us that we tend to be afraid of all the wrong things. Kierkegaard thought that 'fear and trembling' was an appropriate response to the big existential choices we face, but complained that people worried more about the loss of 'an arm, a leg, five dollars, a wife, etc.' than they did about 'losing one's self'.[44] Several philosophers have gone so far as to claim that death is nothing to get too worked up about. For Socrates, the irrationality is to worry about something of which we are entirely ignorant. For all we know, death 'may be the greatest blessing that can happen' to us.[45] For Epicurus it's as illogical to worry about not-being after death as it is to think that life was terrible before you were born. Nothing can be bad if there is nothing for it to be bad for.[46] (We are not irrational to want to avoid death, however, because there is a difference between fearing something and preferring for it not to happen.) Common to all these thinkers is the idea that our instinctive emotional reactions may be very poor guides to what should really concern us.

Whether we are wrong to be afraid or simply fearful of the wrong things, we would all do well to question what the proper objects of fear are. If we do so, we might find that most of our anxieties are not fears to be conquered, but distractions to be ignored as far as possible. Rather than worrying about whether our plane will land safely, for instance, we ought to think more about what kind of life we're going to live if it does. What should be feared more than dying is never to have truly lived.

It might be objected that this is all very well, but reason can't change the way you feel. I find it surprising that so many people take this to be a truism, when it's obvious that we change how we feel about people and things all the time on the basis of what we come to know or think about them. The thought of an intensive farm cage can change your response to a chicken nugget from one of salivation to disgust. People feel very differently about their partners if they discover they've been cheating on them.

Recognising the proper place of emotions does not mean becoming slaves to them. Even when we can't change how we feel, we can use reason to decide how to act on an emotion. And we need to use this capacity if we are to be moral creatures. It's not incidental that none of the world's great moral philosophies have much to say about expressing how you feel. Rather, they ask us to focus on how *other people* feel, on what our duties are, and on what actions would bring about the best situation for as many people as possible. To do this it might be necessary to control our own feelings, something that very much goes against the *zeitgeist*. But to insist that we should always allow our emotions to come to the surface and run their course is to prioritise how we should feel over what we should do. This is the victory of narcissism over morality.

You only need to think about when a stiff upper lip is most admired to recognise that it can be a moral virtue, not an emotional failure. We admire people who control their feelings in order to minimise the extent to which others are forced to share their suffering. Such self-sacrifice is based on the truth that a problem shared is often just a problem doubled. We also admire people who plough on in difficult circumstances doing good work, rather than allowing their own psychic pain to stop them in their tracks.

Pascal is another philosopher who made the mistake of seeing reason and emotion in conflict, one that is more like espionage than warfare, since 'the heart has its reasons of which reason knows nothing'.[47] That might be true, but we should strive to make it the exception rather than the rule. The heart and the head both have their reasons, and they work best when they share them with each other, the heart providing empathy and motivation, and the head making its considered judgements about what feelings to act on, control or challenge. Emotions do not generally need to be either tamed or given free rein, but brought into a fruitful alliance with reason.

The Shrink

——◦◦◦——

There are many verbs we can use in relation to our emotions: accept, express, change, embrace, conquer, control. But 'emotion' is an umbrella term that can cover a lot of different things, and there can be a mismatch between the feelings we have and what we do about them. Sometimes emotions are best expressed and sometimes curbed, for instance. Most people would probably agree that it would be wrong to repress feelings of love simply because it involves giving up some control; and that it would be equally wrong for someone not to control the anger that gets them into fights.

Our thinking about emotions can get muddled, drawing as it does on different traditions and disciplines. One is our Freudian legacy. Many Freudian assumptions have slipped into our ways of thinking unnoticed – dare I say it, unconsciously. In Freud's 'hydraulic' model, bottling up emotions is just bad for our health. 'I don't get angry', says Woody Allen in *Manhattan*, 'I grow a tumour instead'.

Be it the influence of Freud, Nietzsche, or the Sixties, emotional expression has much more value for us nowadays than the ability to keep our feelings in check. We celebrate emotions, regarding them as almost beyond assessment or challenge: 'That's just how I feel.' On the other hand it's easy to see that too much celebration can end in disaster, and that emotions can be inappropriate, excessive or ill-fitting. Many of us will have had the experience of being on the receiving end of someone's unreasonable anger, for instance, or of harbouring feelings of jealousy that we ourselves regard as unwarranted.

Nevertheless, talk of controlling emotions can evoke fears of a stiff-upper-lipped, buttoned-up existence in which the advantage of being able to withstand tremendous trials is obtained at the price of the ability to love, or cry. While it's certainly handy to stay cool in a crisis, most people would probably prefer a life that's a bit of an emotional rollercoaster to one of stunted feelings.

But do we really have to choose between repressing our emotions and being at their mercy? As Aristotle knew, it's possible to feel deeply *and* manage our feelings when inappropriate or excessive if we reclaim the virtue of appropriate self-control. Demanding too much emotional control means potentially missing out on enriching life experiences for fear of being overwhelmed by strong feelings. Having too little control, on the other hand, means being unable to handle the times when acting on our fear or anger or desire would not be conducive to a good life.

These issues show up all the time in daily life, when we find ourselves grappling with troubling emotions like fear, anger, jealousy, even the intoxication of love. Our challenge is to work out when these feelings are pointing us to the truth and when they are telling us lies, when to trust them and when to avoid acting on them.

Monitoring and questioning our responses and leaps of the heart can help us to switch from an instinctive, partial appraisal of the situation to a more rounded and rational one. None of this involves any denial. We can be mindful of an emotion and accept we are feeling it while at the same time being fully aware that it's excessive or out of place. If that happens we can endeavour to change our perspective, our actions, or both.

Fear is a good example of a potentially troublesome emotion. We may or may not be able at any given time to get ourselves to see things in a different way, to convince ourselves there's nothing to be afraid of (if that is indeed the case), but not all is lost if we can't.

Back in the 1990s, Susan Jeffers published a self-help book whose title, *Feel The Fear And Do It Anyway*, has endured in popular memory. Her message was that fear is a normal part of life, and that we would be wrong to take any feelings of anxiety as warnings to avoid the things we are anxious about. Instead, embracing our fears, we should throw ourselves into the jobs, relationships, journeys that are causing those anxieties.

There are good reasons to follow her advice. If we want to do something but are apprehensive about it, waiting until we feel differently might be misguided: making a dent in that kind of feeling is difficult, and we might wait for ever. So we do it anyway. The idea that changing how we act is one of the most effective ways to change how we think and feel is, after all, a cornerstone of the Cognitive-Behaviour therapies. And in the Twelve Steps tradition of Alcoholics Anonymous there is a saying that 'It's easier to act your way into sober thinking than think your way into sober acting'.

Should we always push ourselves to conquer fear? Surely not: clearly there are times when it's crucial to listen to its alarm call. Even Jeffers made the point that her advice did not extend to things that were highly risky or morally dubious. Just as always staying within our comfort zone is not advisable, it should not be a dogma that we must always force ourselves out of it.

But while anxiety about setting off up a mountain in a blizzard might be an easy example of a fear to heed, many others lie in a grey area. It's not always easy to judge how rational our fears are, and whether the feared action is important enough to want to do it anyway. A useful diagnostic question we could borrow from Acceptance and Commitment Therapy (ACT) is whether the proposed action will take us towards what we value in life.

ACT has an unusually enlightened take on dealing with negative emotions. Focusing on getting rid of these is seen as unrealistic and potentially counterproductive. What we need to do is learn to accept all our feelings – like being willing to allow in unwanted guests at a party, instead of spending all our energy trying to keep them out – and start acting on what we believe in. Even if the fear – or other relevant negative emotion – refuses to budge, at least we will have done what we valued, never mind how we felt at the time. Morita Therapy has a concept for this: *arugamama*

– literally 'as it is' in Japanese – which refers to the attitude of accepting the ebbing and flowing of our feelings while we take constructive action. Emotions are often likened to a rollercoaster that takes us on a ride beyond our control. Perhaps it would be better to think of them as tides that we can ride with more or less skill.

WHAT SHOULD YOU BE PROUD OF?

The Sage

<hr>

Pride lives a double life as hero and villain. It's condemned as a deadly sin one minute, promoted as an essential virtue the next. It's blamed for making people haughty and arrogant and praised for enabling oppressed people to stand tall. It's good to take pride in your work but bad to be too proud of what you have achieved.

There is, however, unity in this diversity. All forms of pride involve a kind of pleasure we get when we make a positive appraisal of something whose qualities reflect on us. This invites at least two questions. First, if appropriate pride is taking the right amount of pleasure in good things that we have done, what is modesty and why should it be prized? Second, how can it be that we often derive our pride from the merit of others, even when our own contributions are minimal or non-existent?

It's a cliché of both British soap operas and Mafia movies that at some point a character will declare their pride in the family name. When that family is renowned for its violence or criminality, such blood-is-thicker-than-water loyalty is absurd. But on other occasions, a family shares a set of values that are rightly celebrated, such as hospitality or kindness to strangers. As long as we genuinely share these values and live them, pride in family can be legitimately based on a mutual association around something good.

Feeling proud of others reflects the extent to which we are social animals whose identity always comes in part from the groups we belong to as well as our own atomised essence. We might rightly feel chuffed because people or organisations we value highly are happy to be associated with us, not because we take credit for their achievements. In that sense, taking pride in others can be rooted in genuine humility rather than vanity.

Misplaced pride in others arises when this sense of sharing values is bogus or unwarranted in some way. I can't help but think, for example, that football fans' pride in their clubs is hugely misguided. The direction of the relationship is too one-way, from supporter to team, for any glory to reflect back. Pride in country is also empty when that country doesn't in fact manifest the values you associate with it, or you don't live the values manifest in the country. We can take pride in others only when we participate with them, and they with us, in what it is we are proud of.

What then of modesty? I think modesty will always be problematic just as long as it's taken to be the opposite of pride. Go back to my definition of pride as involving a kind of pleasure we get when we make a positive appraisal of something whose qualities reflect on us. If modesty is understood in contrast to this, it could mean one of three things (or a combination of them).

First, modesty might be thought to be the refusal to

take pleasure from something whose qualities reflect on us, such as an achievement. Looked at in this light, modesty looks like a kind of mistake, a failure to take due credit for what you have done. Perhaps that is why people are often wary of what they perceive to be false modesty: they suspect that the person who downplays her successes is doing so in order to appear virtuous, rather than because she truly believes her achievements are not noteworthy.

Second, we might think that what others would take pride in is not really so good after all. But this would not be true modesty, simply the judgement that one has nothing to be proud of. It makes no sense to be modest about something that is no real achievement at all. You can be humble about a failure, but not modest about it.

Third, modesty might be a rejection of the idea that what is good reflects in any way on us. But again, this doesn't seem to fit what modesty is supposed to be. If we really deserve no credit, we are not being modest by pointing this out, simply honest enough to acknowledge that neither pride nor modesty is appropriate.

Genuine modesty therefore remains elusive, redundant, sometimes turning into a misguided rejection or a disingenuous disguise of pride, sometimes evaporating into thin air.

There is one way, however, that we can make sense of modesty, not as the opposite of pride, but simply as its most truthful form. On this reading, modesty is really just appropriate pride. Take as an example a paradigm of modesty, Paul Rusesabagina, the Rwandan hotel manager who in 1994 took in 1,268 of his countrymen, saving them from his country's genocide. So it's extraordinary that he should entitle his autobiography *An Ordinary Man*. If this isn't modesty, then what is?

This modesty, however, is not incompatible with a certain amount of pride. Rusesabagina surely does get some sense of satisfaction in having done the right thing in difficult circumstances. What keeps him modest is a recognition that, nonetheless, if he takes an honest look at himself, he should not take too much credit for this. Why not? Mainly because he sees the role of 'constitutive luck' in his ability to deal with the situation. Our successes often owe themselves at least in part to the kinds of people we are and the natural abilities we have, neither of which is entirely, even mostly, chosen. In Rusesabagina's case, what really enabled him to do what he did was that he was able to use his charm to keep militia leaders at bay. As he puts it: 'I was a good-natured fellow with the guests who came into the hotel, no matter if they were good friends or odious hate mongers. This was my nature. ... And so when evil dropped by for a drink I was able to have a conversation.'[48]

In other words, Rusesabagina became the hero of the hour because of qualities that he just happened to have, which might be reprehensible in other circumstances. Like Oskar Schindler, he had a willingness to flatter and socialise with the greedy and powerful that would normally leave a bitter taste in the mouth, but in this particular situation was exactly what was needed.

Modesty is then simply the kind of pride that stands out because it involves an exceptionally honest assessment of the real credit that one is due. It does not require us to downplay our achievements, only to not up-play our role in them.

There are perhaps two other added ingredients that contribute to the admirably modest person. First, given that it's difficult to truly know how much credit one is due, the modest person will surely err on the side of giving herself too little credit, not too much. Second, irrespective of the pride one feels, it's entirely right that we should sometimes downplay this in conversation, to avoid presenting ourselves as better than other people or making ourselves the centre of attention. In this sense, modesty isn't always about how you feel, it's about how you behave.

Although he denied it, Churchill is reported to have said of his rival Clement Attlee that he was 'a modest man who has a good deal to be modest about'. The proud would take such a remark as a jibe, but the truly modest would see it simply as a fair description of the facts.

The Shrink

If you want to get on in the world, you'd better get a taste for shouting how great you are. Far away from the old virtue of self-deprecation, self-promotion is now expected, even necessary. We are constantly encouraged to talk up our qualities and achievements in almost every walk of life, from writing CVs to profiles on dating websites. Modesty doesn't really do it anymore: how do you expect to get customers/clients/a lover if you're shy to sell yourself? Could you be a little more upbeat?

In some ways this is good. Many of us find it difficult to acknowledge our qualities and achievements, and a little push to take stock of things we may otherwise easily overlook won't hurt. We all want to have something to be proud of. Feeling there is nothing we can take credit for in life can be a real cause of unhappiness and dissatisfaction, as if we were just a worthless drone.

But we have to be careful, for there is a problematic side to this culture that isn't always obvious. While people may well be cheered by acknowledging the good things about themselves and what they've done, there is a danger of becoming too proud of what we are, in a way that distorts reality and does nothing to promote a flourishing life.

Nor is this simply a moralistic concern. Excessive pride can seamlessly lead to vanity, and when vanity gets its claws into us it leads to overestimating ourselves and growing so attached to an unrealistic idea of who we are that we become unable to acknowledge weaknesses, dependence, flaws. We talk of someone being 'a proud person', who can't recognise mistakes or ask for help. These patterns of thought and behaviour are ultimately detrimental to our well-being. It's this kind of pride we most need to guard against.

The practice of repeating positive affirmations, for instance, a favourite tool of the self-help industry, could encourage the acquisition of such an inflated self-view. Telling ourselves we are beautiful, successful, charismatic and deserving of all good things may or may not have the desired effect – serious doubts have been raised about the efficacy of the practice. But, worse than not working, it could actually hinder meaningful relationships. If we bolster our self-image by creating an armour of positivity around ourselves, we may be less open to others and less agreeable to be around. For instance, we may be so keen to 'avoid negative people' that we become less caring towards our friends or willing to lend an ear.

There are a couple of ways in which we could tweak our outlook to avoid falling into the arms of excessive pride and vanity. One is to appreciate the role that chance plays in our lives. In our eagerness to see ourselves as creators of our destiny, we often discount the sheer luck that has contributed to our good things and achievements. Being aware of the grounds out of which our fortunate circumstances arose is a good counterbalance.

As an exercise in raising our awareness of the interdependence of all things, Vietnamese Zen teacher Thich Nhat Hanh suggests listing and examining both the most significant achievements and the worst failures of your life. Start with the achievements. Reflect on your talents and capacities; on your belief that you are the main cause for your success and on the complacency and arrogance it has produced; on the favourable conditions that led to that success. Similarly for the failures: reflect on your talents and capacities; on your belief that you are incapable of being successful and the difficulties this has caused; on the absence of favourable conditions that led to the failures.

He suggests shedding 'the light of interdependence on the whole matter to see that the achievement is not really yours but the convergence of various conditions beyond your reach', and that 'failures cannot be accounted for by your inabilities but rather by the lack of favorable conditions'.[49] This is meant to encourage us to let go of the self-centred belief that our success and failure begins and ends with us; not, of course, to justify a lazy shedding of responsibility and blaming of outside circumstances.

It's also useful to reflect on what we can legitimately be proud of. Clearly, this does not include things that have fallen in our lap through no effort of our own. As has been said, a horse should not be proud of its beautiful mane. But then we may be equally wrong in believing that the only legitimate source of pride is having done great things, widely acknowledged to be outstanding – getting an MBA or a top job, or climbing a mountain. We can put pride back into the normal and everyday.

We should be most proud of the effort we've made to bring something about, somehow exceeding ourselves, regardless of how big or small the results are. A person who manages to complete a degree while working full-time and raising young children, for instance, has as much right to feel pride as someone who has created a business empire.

We could also be proud of performing a task with care and attention, to the best of our ability, irrespective of how arduous it is or how much appreciation we are likely to get for it. We can take good care of the place we live in, whether it's a palace or a hut. In this case our pride is not an assessment of how brilliant we are, but instead concerns our approach to the work to be done. This kind of pride in how we do things, in our effort or attitude, is positive and need not involve any grandiose, immodest self-appraisal.

GUT FEELINGS AND INTUITIONS

The Shrink

❦

What do you do when you have a decision to make? Do you write a careful list of pros and cons, short-term and long-term, critically examining each of them? Or do you follow your heart/intuition/gut instinct? On the surface, these two main ways we have of processing information – conscious, analytic and reasoned, or quick, automatic and intuitive – couldn't look more different.

Each has its supporters, but the rational system has lost a lot of ground in recent years, while gut feelings, intuitions and hunches of all stripes have found many champions. One of the principal contributors to this tidal wave was neurologist Antonio Damasio, whose research led him to conclude that if a part of the brain dedicated to processing emotion is impaired, decision-making also suffers.[50] The traditional view that feelings hindered rational reflection turned out to be just wrong: in fact, they were essential to it.

We now know that every time we are drawn to something or recoil from it, our brain has been hard at work before we even begin to think consciously about the situation. All our instincts and experience are recruited to produce a gut feeling, a judgement of some kind bubbling up from who knows where. This unconscious processing enables us to read people's intentions and make predictions on the basis of mere fragments of information.

It has become common knowledge that when we meet someone for the first time or go to see a house we are thinking of buying we make up our mind in around two seconds. In *Blink*, Malcolm Gladwell strongly supports the idea that snap judgements and first impressions are often more useful than lengthy analysis (although he doesn't use the word 'intuition', preferring 'rapid cognition').

But is intuition really the bountiful goddess it's sometimes portrayed to be? Many studies have shown that instant judgement isn't always terribly reliable. Gladwell acknowledges this: as he explains on his website, his own survey of hundreds of American companies revealed that most CEOs were tall, suggesting that we irrationally tend to associate height with leadership qualities.

The brain is subject to an extraordinary array of biases and flaws, and at any given time we could be responding to unexamined impulses and prejudices rather than truthful perceptions. Social psychology research on implicit attitudes, for instance, has shown that gender and race stereotypes can exist well below the level of conscious awareness. Intuitions could be picking up on something important or merely betraying unconscious biases.

So although it's important to make good use of our fast-track unconscious information-processing, we shouldn't embrace the wisdom of intuition uncritically. Both the rational and the emotional systems are essential to decision-making. What matters is knowing when to rely on one or the other.

But how do we guard from misleading gut feelings? With difficulty. One phenomenon to learn from is 'expert intuition', whereby for instance a chess master can see what position a player is in just by looking at the board. Although this is an automatic judgement and not the result of a process of deliberation, it's actually based on years of stored thought and experience. Likewise, our own snap judgements are more likely to be reliable in domains where we have acquired some expertise. We could give some thought to what these are, remembering that even experts don't always get it right.

Our track record is also relevant. If you're always losing on the horses, you probably shouldn't believe your 'intuition' that this time you've got the right one. If, on the other hand, you have tended to have successful hunches about business opportunities, say, perhaps you don't need to be so wary of trusting them. Of course there's no guarantee.

It's worth paying attention to our intuitions, but it's also important to remember that instant judgements have many sources – natural instincts, habits and assumptions we've acquired, culturally-determined prejudices, knacks learned from experience. Each needs to be examined through the lens of reason.

Some general habits of mind can help. It's a good idea to get used to regularly monitoring our responses, double-checking our facts and options, questioning our assumptions and inferences, asking ourselves whether we are being too led by what we want to believe and whether there are alternative interpretations of the situation.

Some of the more 'actuarial' decision-making methods can also help. Instead of simply listing the reasons for and against a particular course of action, we could interrogate them, protecting those that express genuine values and eliminating spurious ones. We could also try to weight the reasons, ordering them by importance. While this is far from an exact science, it can help us to get a sense of their relative importance.

We should certainly give a place to hunches and snap judgements, as they could be detecting something important. But this does not mean supplanting critical reasoning, as there is always the danger of falling prey to some kind of cognitive distortion. Gut feelings work best in dialogue with rational reflection. It's not a question of head versus heart, more like an ongoing head–heart dialogue.

The Sage

Imagine that you have abandoned a sinking ship in a lifeboat. You see someone drowning a few metres away. There is room in the boat and plenty of emergency supplies. What should you do?

You'd be very odd if you tried to answer this question by a process of rigorous rational deliberation. Almost everyone has a very clear moral intuition: steer the boat over and save the drowning passenger. But as the philosopher Onora O'Neill points out, we can draw out from that one specific intuition a more general moral principle: those with means should make relatively small efforts to save those who do not, and that applies as much to affluent Westerners in relation to people in the developing world as it does to people fleeing a sinking ship.[51]

What might seem odd about this line of reasoning is that intuition seems to be doing all the heavy philosophical lifting. All we've done is elicit a gut response, and then extrapolate a general principle from it. This is not, however, untypical of how moral philosophy works. In some cases, an entire literature can grow up around a series of thought experiments and the intuitions they elicit. Most famously, or perhaps notoriously, there is the 'trolley problem', where a runaway train is heading into a tunnel where it will kill a number of people working on the line. You can reduce the death toll, but only by making others victims: by diverting the trolley with a switch onto a line where fewer workers will be killed; stopping it in its tracks by pushing a fat man off a bridge to block it; dumping said rotund gentleman on the line by means of opening up a trap door beneath his feet; and so on and so on. 'Trolleyology', as it has mockingly become known, compares the different intuitions elicited by variations on the set-up and tries to see if these point to morally important differences or simply inconsistencies in our values.

Daniel Dennett calls such thought experiments 'intuition pumps' to make it clear that they are not arguments, simply means of drawing out our gut feelings in ways that make them clear and transparent.[52] Nevertheless, there is a real problem in explaining precisely what role these intuitions should then play in our moral reasoning. Often it seems to be a crucial one. When moral intuitions clash with moral principles, for example, that is more often taken as a reason to question the principle than to dump the intuition.

If we are to put intuitions in their proper place, we need to be clear about what they are. It is sometimes assumed that intuitions are innate, but in fact there is no reason to suppose we are born with them. Some may be natural instincts, some may have been acquired through life experience. However we acquired them, they lead us to make automatic, often strong, judgements in the absence of any conscious, rational deliberation, and sometimes even in direct contradiction to such calculations. If we are asked to rationally justify an intuition, we may not be able to do so, and even when we are, if we were honest we would notice that what we are actually doing is rationalising after the event, *post facto*. The rational argument may indeed justify the intuition, but it's not because of the argument that we have the intuition, or feel that it's the right one.

Intuitions of this kind are not only important in ethics. Arguably they are integral to almost all, if not all, forms of rational inquiry. For example, one of the oldest questions in philosophy is: What is knowledge? And one of the oldest answers is: Justified true belief. This can be challenged, however, by rolling out an intuition-pumping thought experiment. Your neighbour has a white Mini Cooper. You look out of your front window across the road and see it parked outside their house, where lights are on and silhouettes move behind curtains. So you are justified in believing that your neighbours are at home, which indeed they are. If this isn't knowledge, then what is? However, as it happens, your neighbours have only been home for five minutes. For the four hours before that, other family members were in the house, and one of these had parked her white Mini Cooper, which looks identical to your neighbour's, outside. So had you opened your window then you would have concluded that your neighbours were home for what seem to be exactly the same reasons, but you would have been wrong. So the fact that your justified belief turns out to be true appears to be a matter of luck. In such cases, surely you can't be said to have knowledge?

When considering a question like this, intuition again seems to play an important role. Many people have a strong sense that the thought experiment shows you didn't have knowledge after all. But if asked to explain why, reasons will be found *post facto* and will not necessarily be what really grounds that judgement. Reason justifies but intuition verifies.

Does this mean ethics and all sorts of other forms of reasoning are nothing more than the process of providing a respectable rational veneer for what are really just brute feelings? Hopefully not. Relying on our gut feelings is not the same as entirely trusting whatever we intuitively feel. For instance, reason can expose some intuitions as unjustifiable prejudices or irrational distortions. Even if we can't help having such automatic reactions, we can then change what we go on to do on the basis of them.

Nevertheless, it's important to accept that reason cannot do without intuitive judgement altogether. The project of becoming more rational is to minimise the extent to which we rely exclusively on intuition while recognising that we can't eliminate it altogether. Even if you think that I've overstated the case, it's surely true that in the realm of pragmatic deliberation, intuitive judgements are in practice, if not in theory, always going to have to do some work. At the most basic level, we simply don't always have the time to think things through with the thoroughness that pure reason would demand. Intuition is therefore not an alternative to reason, but its indispensable accomplice.

CONTRARY TO APPEARANCES?

The Shrink

❧

It seems to be a chicken-and-egg thing: if we value ourselves we'll take care of our body and if we take care of our body we'll value ourselves more. Looking after our body is commonly regarded not only as an expression of positive self-regard, but also as a way of boosting it. It makes sense: we are a mind-body unit, so it would be surprising if there were no correlations between states of mind and states of the body. Tweaking something at any level may well lead to changes elsewhere in the system.

But could it be that the relationship between the two is less straightforward than we tend to think? Not many would agree with the view of the Greek Cynics that the only thing that matters is reason and therefore we shouldn't concern ourselves with our bodies or our appearance at all. But less extreme versions of this – to the effect that the body is just a shell containing our soul and shouldn't be granted undue attention – are definitely still in circulation.

Sure, few would advise neglecting health and hygiene. But the views that advocate disregarding the body perhaps have more purchase in relation to appearance. Why should we care whether we are having a good or a bad hair day, whether our skin is wrinkled, whether our clothes and accessories convey the right messages about who we are? Surely what matters is our character, our values and interests, how we treat others?

It's certainly true that when people have zest for life and are at ease with themselves we often find them attractive regardless of conventional notions of beauty. It's difficult to silence the suspicion that caring too much about appearance is superficial and misguided, and that real beauty comes from within.

But we can't ignore the fact that we are bodies as much as minds. So is there anything to be said in defence of self-beautification? We could start with the fact that the tendency to take pleasure in making ourselves look good is natural and ubiquitous in human cultures. But this will not take us too far. So are lying and cheating. What is natural is not necessarily to be endorsed and encouraged.

There are pragmatic reasons for grooming. We can't help communicating with the world through how we present ourselves, so it's worth giving that some thought. If you turn up at a formal job interview wearing sandals, shorts and a loud tropical shirt, you should be prepared to be surprised if you get the job.

There are also issues of convention and civility to bear in mind, like dressing appropriately for an occasion. Of course this very much depends on whether we want to endorse the particular convention. You may decide dinner jackets are elitist and therefore eschew them even if it puts you at a disadvantage, but be happy to follow social customs at a funeral.

Another thing to bear in mind is that putting some care into our appearance can change how we feel, and so it could be a valid form of self-intervention. Switching from wearing black to wearing bright colours, for instance, may well improve our mood. There may be times when recovering a lost pride in our appearance might provide the kind of boost we need to work on all sorts of other life-changing developments.

So we may allow that a degree of interest can play a positive role in our life and does not have to mean becoming Prada fiends, hiding behind layers of carefully applied make-up. But how can we work out what is appropriate and what is excessive?

There are signs to look out for: we are clearly too concerned about our looks, for instance, if we allocate most of our time and resources to the care of the body, neglecting more worthwhile pursuits; or when our sense of who we are is so dependent on how we appear to others that we can't face the world without wearing a mask. A report of the American Psychological Association pointed to research showing that girls' confidence and comfort in their own bodies was undermined by thinking of and treating it as an object of others' desires.[53]

We can also become slaves to oppressive and unrealistic ideals of beauty. There are instances of this all around us. A few years ago a BBC documentary entitled *My Small Breasts and I* followed three young women suffering from varying degrees of distress and dysfunctionality. Their attempts to resolve their issues involved different paths, including unusual ones such as suction cups and phototherapy. Were all that time and emotional energy really well spent?

Another widespread ideal is the imperative to look forever young. Plastic surgery, for instance, raises strong feelings in both advocates and opponents. 'Why not?', say the former. After all, it's only an extension of our ordinary self-care, and it could make our daily life a lot easier, especially if we work in an environment where youthful looks are demanded.

But the list of reasons against seems much weightier. The costs and unexpected risks of surgery alone should be off-putting enough. The objection that we should not go along with an ethos that puts youth on a pedestal is not insignificant. But perhaps the most substantial is that trying too hard is ultimately counterproductive. No matter how many nips and tucks we indulge in, age will always have the last laugh. We had better prepare, therefore, by investing in alternative sources of satisfaction rather than engaging in a desperate struggle to sustain this one.

Although there may be such a thing as appropriate caring about our looks, there is no neat line separating it from excessive concern. That's often the case in life. Away from the extremes, excess can be judged only in relation to a particular person and situation. We need to learn to draw our own lines depending on the function these things play in our life, in our own mental economy and daily relationships.

For every person whose dishevelled appearance reflects a disordered mind, there is another whose suffering is hidden behind neatly coiffured, colour-coordinated looks. Getting a haircut, improved hygiene, paying more attention to clothing might be the first step towards recovery for one. For another, progress might mean daring to walk to the shops with no make-up on.

So it's not really a question of what we should or shouldn't do – wear lipstick, or Manolos. What matters is reflecting on the meaning such self-care has for us and the role it plays in our life.

The Sage

Appearances make hypocrites of us all. Virtually everyone agrees that we shouldn't judge people on their looks but we all do just that, whether we admit it or not. Psychologists have shown that even people who spend their lives working against prejudice are affected by stereotypes of gender, race and even forenames, which can be subtle indicators of social class.

If you think you're immune to these biases, then go online and take the Harvard Implicit Association Test.[54] Without giving too much away, unless you are very unusual indeed, you will find that you intuitively associate certain qualities and attributes according to stereotypes that you will consciously reject. For instance, you may sincerely believe that women are as capable of being scientists as men – indeed you may be a woman who thinks this – and yet almost certainly a man will come to mind more easily and quickly when you come across the word 'scientist' than a woman. You will also be more likely to attribute positive qualities such as intelligence and kindness to those with attractive faces than to the ugly.

Given how entrenched superficial judgements are, how we should present ourselves creates political as well as personal dilemmas, particularly for women. Conform to expectation and we might be complicit in perpetuating pernicious stereotypes. Defy expectation and the chances are you will pay a price, because no matter what people say, most, if not all, will treat you differently. So, admirable though it may be to resist pressure to present yourself in ways that reinforce prejudice, it's too much to insist that people put their own self-interest on the line in an attempt to buck a system that most defiance would hardly even scratch.

We can, however, become too sanguine about the need to accept the world for what it is, rather than challenging it. Consider, for instance, the fact that many find taking care of the way they look helps boost their self-esteem. That may be true, but there are many bad things that can also shore up ego, such as wielding excessive power over others or wallowing in the praise of sycophants. The value of looking good, like anything else, is not measured purely in terms of how it makes us feel.

On the other hand, there is a tendency for the educated to overstate the triviality of surfaces. A disdain for appearances is often taken as a mark of intellectual superiority, an ability to see further and deeper than the shallow masses. But although there is indeed more to most things than meets the eye, it doesn't follow that all that is most real and important is hidden from view. Yet this is in many cases an unexamined assumption, based on a recurring distinction in the history of ideas between appearances and reality.

This contrast is found in its most extreme form in the writings of Plato and Kant. Plato's idea is that everything in the material world is an imperfect copy of an ideal found only in the imperceptible world of forms.[55] Then there is Kant's idea that we can access only the 'phenomenal world' of things as they appear, while the real 'noumenal' world of things as they are is beyond human experience. But even if Plato or Kant are right, the everyday distinction between appearance and reality is one that applies wholly within the material or phenomenal world. So we talk about how someone presents themselves and how they 'really are', but this latter reality has nothing to do with any unknown worlds of forms and noumena. Platonic and Kantian metaphysics therefore does nothing to dignify the appearance/reality distinction as applied to real life.

Rather than think in terms of appearance and reality, we would often do better to think about levels of the one

reality we inhabit. Different levels come to the fore depending on the means of perception or description. Take a ring
donut, for example. At the level of human perception and
everyday description, this is a soft, light, continuous struc-
ture with a hole in the middle. Perceived through an electron microscope and described by physicists, the whole
itself becomes a kind of hole: largely empty space, with
atoms buzzing around it. But that doesn't mean that the
human-level description is a 'mere appearance'. Both levels
are real, and which one it makes sense even for a physicist
to talk about depends on whether the donut is the object
of research or fuel for the researcher.

Nonetheless, people often say that science shows us that
objects do not appear to us as they really are. In this they
are buying into a general principle that is also often taken
to be the lesson of Plato and Kant: that what is usually hidden is more real than that which is usually visible. But if
you think about that for even a short while, it just doesn't
make sense. You wouldn't say, for example, that each time
you open up a Russian doll, the one you reveal is more real
than the one it sits in. They are all equally real. In the same
way, the mere fact that objects and people are 'nested' in
some way, from the micro to the macro, tells you nothing
about which layer contains the greatest reality.

This has significance for how we appear both physically and personally. You cannot assume that how someone looks reflects less of how they really are than how they
think, not least because how they look might be a direct

result of how they think. Most obviously, the way people present themselves can say a lot about what their values really are, things that they may not even realise themselves.

But perhaps the point about levels of reality is most important when it comes to countering the kind of cod-Freudianism that always assumes what is absent from consciousness is somehow more indicative of who we really are than that which is usually present. So when a normally calm person shows extreme anger, people mutter that they are now showing their true colours. But there is no reason to assume this. Why not simply say that even the calmest person has the capacity for rage? If we do open up a kind of placid Russian doll and find an angrier one within, we haven't revealed the true person, only a side of them that is both smaller and usually well contained.

Contrary to appearances, then, appearances can be as real as anything else. Reality is layered, the visible no more or less real than the invisible. The wise, therefore, appreciate the truths in appearances, not just the truths behind them.

WILL AND RESOLUTION

The Sage

I don't think it's a great puzzle of the universe that you can't make toast in a kettle. Anyone who spent hours trying to brown slices of bread with one would be rightly dismissed as a crank. I feel somewhat the same way towards philosophers who think there is a really deep problem about weakness of will. While they sit around scratching their heads asking, 'How can it be that we don't do what we think we ought to do?', I look on and think: 'You should get out more.' Sure, it would be a puzzle if purely logical, rule-following machines routinely gave up without good reason, but no observer of human behaviour should see weakness of will as anything other than entirely natural.

This is one issue where psychology really should have taken over the job from philosophy long ago. It is now very clear that the human mind does not have a single control centre and that conflicting, contradictory desires are to be expected. It's as though different voices in our heads are calling for different things and the one that gets its way is usually not the most reasonable, or even the one that has held the floor the longest, but simply the one that's shouting loudest at the crucial moment of decision. So rather than weakness of will being the paradox of an individual doing other than what she really wants, it's better described as doing other than what she on balance most wants, and there is no logical contradiction in that. It's normal to behave differently when you're off-balance.

However, psychology leaves at least a morsel for philosophy in the intriguing suggestion by Stephen P. Schwartz that, from a logical point of view, there are many times when it is strength of will, not weakness, that looks rationally puzzling.[56] Take giving up smoking. Say you've had a twenty-a-day habit for decades and you want to give up. You pick the time, you pick the day, and then a paper tube stuffed with tobacco implores you to smoke it. Would it really make any difference if you heeded the call? In the grand scheme of things, one more won't hurt. That's not illogical, it's just true. And, of course, that will also be true of the next one, and the next one, and the next one …

If you want to give up, there has to be a last smoke, of course. The problem is that there is never a good reason why any particular cigarette should be it. So it looks like it's never irrational to have just one more and there is never any rational reason why any given cigarette should be the last one. The same is true for one more glass of wine, one last bit of cake, another day of not going to the gym.

I think the solution is that, in order to achieve certain goals, we sometimes have to make arbitrary choices about which particular steps we take to get to them. It doesn't matter if this or that cigarette is the last one, as long as one of them is. Similarly, no particular piece of cake will ruin our diet but we must spurn enough of them or else we'll never lose weight. Hence, paradoxically, we find we do have good reasons to commit to a set of actions, each of which we individually have no good reasons to do at all. That's quite a difficult thought to get your head around, and few manage to get that far with their reasoning. So rather than being irrational creatures who allow their hot desires to overrule what cooler reason tells them is in their best interests, the weak-willed are people for whom a limited amount of logic is more troublesome than none at all.

Philosophers are not the only ones who get weakness of will wrong. Common sense suggests that the biggest problem we face with resolutions is sticking to them. I would suggest that our problem is really that we don't have a clear enough idea of when we should give up. The advice of Homer Simpson is appealing but probably not the wisest: 'You tried your best and failed miserably. The lesson is: never try.' Nonetheless, you should not always persist in trying indefinitely. Wisdom requires knowing when to give up, and although Kenny Rogers and Aristotle make for an unlikely duo, together they tell you pretty much all you need to know about this.

Aristotle's most enduring and useful insight was that virtues are not simply good things, the more of which we have the merrier, but are actually the right amount of things that we can have too much or too little of. Determination is the perfect example. Too little, and you are weak and irresolute. Too much, and you're inflexible, blinkered or fanatical. Just right is the eponymous gambler of the Kenny Rogers song, who is able to look at the cards he's got, know when to hold 'em and when to fold 'em.

What gives this gambler his wisdom? What he always has to do is to weigh up the value of the cards in his hand against the value of those he thinks others might be holding, and the stake on the table. To do this, he always has to be aware of how the situation can change as new information comes to light. A risk worth taking becomes reckless when the stakes rise too high. What looks like a good hand can come to seem better or worse if you get a better idea of what your opponent might have. The most elementary mistake a gambler can make is simply to turn over the cards, decide they are good or bad, and resolve to either fold now or hold until the bitter end.

In real life, whether we're working with the hand we've been dealt or cards we have chosen freely for ourselves, the same basic principles apply. When we set out to achieve something, it's because we have decided, at least implicitly, that the hand we hold is worth playing to win. But once we get started, reality has a habit of telling us that our initial calculations were wrong. We might continue to value what we seek just as much, but come to realise that the price of achieving it rises too high. Perhaps most importantly, that price includes the opportunity costs of the things we are *not* doing in our determination to stick it out. Think of all the sailing you could have been doing all those weekends you dedicated to completing your matchstick model of the *Cutty Sark*.

Plato believed that no one who was really convinced that a course of action was right would ever choose to do anything else.[57] If he was correct, then weakness of resolution could be a sign of weakness of conviction. The other side of the coin is that we can have too much resolution when our conviction remains the same despite the facts, or our knowledge of them, changing. What's most needed then is the clarity, not the courage, of our convictions.

The Shrink

When we set resolutions that are in some way hard to achieve we often find ourselves backsliding at the first obstacle. Alternatively we keep going long after the goal's use-by date, effectively pursuing what is a dead goal for fear of being a quitter. People get tied up in knots trying to decide whether to stick to things they've decided. They reflect for hours on whether they should make more effort, commit and complete, or follow the line of least resistance and go with the flow – life's too short anyway.

The problem is not any shortage of advice on how to make resolutions that stick. This tends to boil down to a few rules of thumb, such as breaking down ambitious aims into manageable chunks, setting goals that are specific and realistic, telling other people about them, giving ourselves small rewards. But none of this stops us getting entangled in decision-making dilemmas. If you're wondering about giving up a goal, I suggest a line of inquiry that begins with asking yourself whether the goal is right for you. If it is, bind yourself to it. If it isn't, give it up.

The first step is to reflect on whether the resolution is right for us at this time anyway. Too often we set a goal without doing enough hard thinking about how valuable it is for us, or whether it's worth the effort. Anything that involves going against our temperament or habits is likely to require effort. Sometimes our resolve vanishes as soon as we realise this.

So an unflinching examination of your values is in order. Is there a mismatch between what you actually want and what you think you should want? Have you passively accepted someone else's value system? Do your values clash with one another? Is the goal valuable in itself or only as a means to an end? How important would you rate it on a scale of 0–10? This question in particular will give you some useful information: we might well value learning Latin, say, but simply not enough to be prepared to put in the work when there's so much else to do.

But often there's nothing wrong with the resolution you made. You are satisfied that you really should give up smoking, whichever way you think about it. And you do make a start, full of enthusiasm, but before too long you find yourself falling into your sweet old ways, concluding you just don't have the willpower.

That would be a mistake. Thinking of 'willpower' as an inner ability that we either do or don't have is misleading and counterproductive. The truth is that we do genuinely want something – to produce creative work, or be healthier – but we also want something else, be it pleasure, comfort, or simply not having to make an effort. Never underestimate our reluctance to go against the grain, the insidious power of long-established habits.

Our desires and inclinations can be at odds with each other, some reaching for what we want right now and others more interested in securing our longer-term well-being. The former often win. But if we are clear about the way forward, the next step is to find out where our motivation is really leading us and look for more effective strategies to redirect it.

Easier said than done. In my years of working with addictions I realised there are two main gremlins to guard against. One is acting quickly and without reflection: you have a sudden urge while you are passing by the cupcakes and immediately buy one, devouring it straight away. The other is rationalising: for instance, deceiving yourself into thinking it's OK to make an exception just for today (it's your birthday, or you're particularly stressed).

This is where how we think about willpower matters. In the *Odyssey*, Ulysses knew he couldn't resist the lure of the sirens just by gritting his teeth, and therefore asked his sailors to tie him to the ship's mast. His willpower consisted precisely in enlisting outside help to stop him acting on what he realised he would feel like doing in the future. In our more ordinary circumstances, we can still find ways to tie ourselves to the mast by putting temptation out of reach, or making a binding commitment we can't escape from. We can outsmart ourselves only if we look ahead and prepare.

Of course it makes a difference whether you are considering returning to smoking or giving up a PhD. In the first case it's easier to see clearly that the resolution is right, to see past the rationalisations that a part of us is busy producing. The second case can be more complicated, the pros and cons more evenly balanced.

Imagine you have been working towards a PhD for several years, struggling with unsympathetic supervisors, your low motivation, the fact that you're neglecting your friends and hobbies. So far, you haven't even considered giving up, but before re-enrolling this year you just wonder whether enough is enough. But you've invested so much in it, and you don't want to be a quitter. You will get there eventually.

Tenacity is of course an essential virtue in life, but its value is so well rehearsed that it ends up being overstated. In fact, stubbornly beavering away at goals that are no longer relevant is no better than giving them up too soon. An important trap to avoid in this respect is basing our decision on how much we have invested in a goal, financially or otherwise. In the case of your PhD, the years of toil and tuition fees paid should be irrelevant. All you need to consider is how much of a priority it is for you right now, not when you started on it.

Of course, if a goal is simply unattainable, the decision to abandon it should be easy enough to make. While it's not uncommon to fail to spot an immovable obstacle, shining a little objectivity on it should reveal it for what it is. The really difficult decisions are the ones that involve ditching projects that are attainable only at a cost to health, relationships or enjoyment of life. And these costs can be very real. As often, there is no algorithm to get us out of this. You will have to reflect on your priorities and decide whether it's worth carrying on. But if the pursuit of a goal is damaging things that are important to you, such as health and relationships, giving up may be the only sensible thing to do.

THE VARIETIES OF SELF-LOVE
WORTH HAVING

The Shrink

~~~~~

One of the pioneers of family therapy, Virginia Satir, found inspiration in a black iron pot she remembered from growing up on a farm in Wisconsin. This pot contained different things at different times: sometimes it was filled with the soap her mother used to make; sometimes with stew for the farm workers; and sometimes with manure for the flower beds. Anybody wanting to use it had to find out what it was now full of, and how full it was. She found this a useful metaphor when discussing her clients' feelings of self-worth. A 'high pot' became shorthand for everything that goes with high self-worth, a 'low pot' for the opposite. What Satir called self-worth is a form of what we could broadly call self-love. Whatever we label it, how we think of it matters. What form of self-love should we aim to fill our pots with?

More often these days we talk about self-esteem, by which we mean some kind of positive self-appraisal. Low self-esteem is diagnosed and self-diagnosed all over the land. It has become an almost unchallenged orthodoxy to blame it for all sorts of evils, while refilling a depleted stock is regarded as a sure way to health and well-being.

So you might try to boost your self-esteem by doing self-affirmations, for instance. You stand in front of the mirror and repeatedly tell yourself how lovable or successful you are, for instance. But drawing attention to the gap between how we would like to be and how we *actually* see ourselves can make us feel worse.

Another dubious strategy is pushing ourselves to achieve more in the hope of our self-esteem following suit. But we can compare this to a leaky pot, one that needs to be replenished all the time to stay full. As soon as you stop adding, the level drops and all of a sudden you're left with no self-esteem.

An excess of self-esteem is no great way to live either, as it can lead us to overreach ourselves and make us haughty towards others. Russ Harris, writing about Acceptance and Commitment Therapy, rightly asks: 'Have you ever tried to build a good-quality relationship, based on openness, respect and equality, with someone hooked on their own positive self-judgements; someone completely fused with "I am a success", "I am a champion" or "I am a winner"?'[58] He also points out that high self-esteem has been found to correlate with undesirable traits like narcissism, prejudice and defensiveness in the face of honest feedback.

And according to psychologist Steven Pinker: 'Perhaps the most extraordinary popular delusion about violence of the past quarter-century is that it is caused by low self-esteem. Self-esteem can be measured, and surveys show that it is the psychopaths, street toughs, bullies, abusive husbands, serial rapists, and hate-crime perpetrators who are off the scale.'[59]

So what should we aim for? It's not just a question of making positive self-judgements, because these should not be divorced from how we act in the world. It's no good trying to puff up our opinion of ourselves without paying attention to our actions: convincing ourselves we're great when our behaviour is selfish and inconsiderate, for instance, or when we know we're not doing our best. No matter how many affirmations we repeat every morning, there is no substitute for doing an honest self-inventory and actually making an effort to be a better person. Unfortunately, such an inventory is likely to include self-criticism as well as praise.

One could say we are self-critical enough, thank you very much. That is true, and is well attested by the wealth of titles catering for those affected: *Master Your Inner Critic*, *Self-therapy for Your Inner Critic*, *Beyond the Inner Critic*, *Coping with Your Inner Critic*, *Disarming your Inner Critic*.

But at the same time social psychology studies suggest that in many ways we're a deluded bunch, not nearly as self-critical as we should be. Most people believe they have above average abilities, and generally suffer from at least some form of self-serving bias. For instance, psychologists have believed for some time that we tend to take credit for our successes and blame external factors for our failures, but when it comes to judging other people's behaviour we are more likely to hold them responsible, ignoring the extenuating power of circumstances.

How can we be so self-critical and yet so deluded? Perhaps we fail to distinguish properly between two types of self-criticism. One is hostility towards oneself, the opposite of which is kindness to self; the other is an unflinching honesty about who we are, the opposite of which is self-delusion. So we could be harsh without being objective and vice versa. Self-criticism in the hostile sense is not conducive to self-improvement. A self-flagellating inner homunculus is not going to help anybody become a better person. But objectivity and self-compassion form a good pair: it's OK to have an inner critic so long as its voice is kindly and rational.

The most appropriate form of self-love, then, is not self-esteem in the sense of having a high opinion of ourselves, but what Buddhists know as loving kindness towards oneself, or what we could call self-acceptance. This is echoed by psychiatrist and cognitive therapist David Burns, who in the classic self-help book *Feeling Good* suggests that a constructive understanding of self-esteem is treating oneself like a beloved friend.

This doesn't mean letting ourselves off all the time. A useful distinction in this respect is offered by psychologist Paul Gilbert: *compassionate self-correction* is a desire to improve, while *shame-based self-attacking* is a desire to punish.[60] And Russ Harris's helpful hint is that there is a significant difference between assessing our *actions*, which is workable, and judging *ourselves*, which is not.[61] Self-acceptance means letting go of global self-judgements about ourselves as human beings, not turning a blind eye to our behaviour and the impact of our actions.

Now, if we can fill our pots with clarity and self-acceptance we will have made a good start towards the kind of self-love worth having.

The Sage

Immanuel Kant defined a categorical imperative as a command that 'represented an action as objectively necessary in itself'. Today, we are bombarded by categorical imperatives, one of the most common being the command to love thyself. Unfortunately, instead of being informed by the austere, systematic thought of Prussian philosophers, this injunction owes more to the ideology of positive thinking, whose gurus range from self-help hucksters to popular singers.

Take, for instance, the command sung by Bing Crosby in Johnny Mercer's 'Ac-Cent-Tchu-Ate the Positive'. Here we find what we might call Bing's Threefold Categorical Imperative: 'Eliminate the negative, / Latch on to the affirmative, / Don't mess with Mister In-Between'. To which the shorter, categorical threefold reply is wrong, wrong, wrong, especially when it comes to how we view ourselves.

First up, let's get rid of this idea that we need to eliminate the negative. This is a deeply anti-philosophical injunction, since philosophy has always thrived on criticism and fault-finding. The Socrates we discover in the dialogues of Plato made a career out of doing very little other than showing people why they were wrong, and the balance in the discipline has remained firmly on the side of the negative ever since.

Negativity gets a bad press these days, but we desperately need the right kind of it. Most of us want to believe what is true rather than what is false. We want to have an accurate picture of the world, not one distorted by wishful thinking, ignorance or prejudice. Yet, if we are honest, most of our beliefs are based on scanty information, hearsay, expert testimony or received opinion. Of course they are: life is literally too short to rigorously examine the bases of all our beliefs. So if we really want our beliefs to be sound, we have to be alert to the ways in which they might be false. We have to nurture an acute inner critic, one that is able to detect reasons for justified doubt and evidence that contradicts what we currently think. This is what the discipline of philosophy fosters above all else.

This critic works best, however, when it's as impersonal and emotion-free as possible. The more people identify a belief as theirs, the less willing they are to consider objectively evidence that contradicts it. It no longer becomes a simple question of whether something is true or false, it becomes about your willingness to give up something of which you feel ownership.

Similarly, if you think too much about whether you are a good or a bad person, it can become harder to consider whether an action is the right or wrong thing to do. Changing our minds might imply judging our past actions harshly, which can easily lead to defence mechanisms coming up with reasons to believe you were right all along.

That's why the best philosophical inner critic is neither nice nor nasty, neither gentle nor harsh. In fact, it's a critic that has nothing to do with you as a person at all. It's all about the beliefs. If that sounds coldly objective, that's because it is, and all the better for it. Philosophy is often accused of being excessively rational, dismissing emotion as irrelevant at best and a harmful distraction at worst. But when it comes to self-criticism, philosophy's alleged vice turns out to be its greatest virtue.

Far from trying to eliminate the negative, we need to nurture the kind of negativity that is clear-sighted and fair. This requires thinking about what is wrong with ourselves and our beliefs rather than feeling that we are awful people. It's neither self-love nor self-hatred, but rational self-judgement. So in place of the kind of positive affirmations commended by so many self-help gurus, I advise looking in the mirror every morning and repeating: 'I am a weak, stupid, pathetic, deluded bald ape, and that's OK. Now, how do I make the best of the comically bad job God made of me?'

To make the best of ourselves, however, we can't afford to be too emotionally indulgent. Accepting ourselves as we are is just the start, from which we need to do some work. I became acutely aware of this a few years ago when I interviewed the conservative English philosopher Roger Scruton. I was struck by a remark he made about the need to 'make ourselves more lovable to each other'.[62] Today's common sense is that everyone deserves to be loved, whoever they are and whatever they do. Latch on to the affirmative. Being loved is a human right and the idea that it's down to you to make yourself worthy of it is absurd.

That certainly seems to be how we usually view self-love. It has become a truism that you cannot love anyone else unless you first learn to love yourself. But even if that is so, it does not follow that your self-love can or should be unearned.

Take as a parallel the message of the 1971 Staples Singers hit 'Respect Yourself'. A laudable imperative, but as the song makes clear, respecting yourself requires you to behave respectfully to others as well. As the first line has it, 'If you disrespect anybody that you run in to, / How in the world do you think anybody's supposed to respect you?' You respect yourself by making yourself worthy of respect. The same is surely true of self-love. Loving yourself irrespective of how much you deserve it is vain, not virtuous.

But isn't unconditional love meant to be the best, purest kind? For God, perhaps. After all, if he created us, with all our weaknesses and failings, he has a duty of paternal benevolence to everyone. For mere mortals, in contrast, unconditional love looks like folly. There may be a kind of generalised good will to all humanity that should be universal, but the love that touches us most deeply does so because it loves us for who we are as individuals. Indiscriminate love has its place, but we can only value and cherish the uniqueness of a person if we appreciate genuinely good qualities they really have.

For self-love to have any value, therefore, we must be able to find things within ourselves that make that love worthy. Scruton was right. Rather than trying to love ourselves, we should simply try to make ourselves lovable, and the rest will follow.

This leaves us with the final element of Bing's Imperative: Don't mess with Mister In-Between. How wrong could he be? Mister In-Between is the philosopher's best friend, someone you should hang out with as much as possible, for he has a lot to teach us. Being constructively self-critical requires taking stock of the negative and the positive, usually with the conclusion that one is neither entirely in the right nor in the wrong. Similarly, if we really do want to make ourselves more worthy of the love of ourselves and others, we need to appreciate those aspects of ourselves that are lovable, those that are not particularly endearing but acceptable, and those we really need to try to change.

Bing's Categorical Imperative therefore needs a thorough rewrite. So, all together now: 'You've got to attenuate the positive, / Accept the negative, / Work on the affirmative, / Team up with Mister In-Between.' Not as catchy, maybe, but it at least has the virtue of being true.

ON SELF-DECEPTION

The Shrink

---❈---

That human beings are able to deceive themselves is clear. The examples are abundant: falsely believing that our spouse is faithful, that our romantic intentions are reciprocated, that we stand a good chance to pass an exam or succeed in a career, that we behaved well in an awkward situation. And believing all these things not only without sound evidence, but with good hints and signs to the contrary, which we should be able to get but somehow manage to overlook. We deceive ourselves about our motives, abilities and prospects all the time, going to great lengths to shield ourselves from painful realisations and maintain our beliefs in comforting untruths.

This has always seemed like a puzzling phenomenon, which raises several questions about how this is possible, whether it's a good or a bad thing, to what extent it can be avoided. Much has been written about all this. But what should we do about it? If we're self-deceived we're by definition ignorant of the fact: why shouldn't we be allowed to bask in our blissful unawareness? If you were deceiving yourself, would you want to know?

There are reasons why we might be tempted to embrace self-deception wholeheartedly. A certain amount of it is probably harmless, and arguably good for us. An over-inflated view of ourselves may help us to pursue more ambitious goals and overcome obstacles. It may create virtuous cycles that increase the likelihood of success. Or it may simply allow us to cope with living without becoming too mired in misery. Several studies have suggested that moderately self-deluded people are happier and more successful, while realism is correlated with depression.

That is no mean advantage. It's almost enough to make us want to become more rather than less self-deceived, even though on the other side lurk dangers like faulty judgements about the world, excessive expectations opening the possibility of extreme disappointment, and catastrophic decision-making.

Even more importantly, it seems there's no way of escaping this self-delusion. We're all ailing with a mild form of it. Most people overrate their abilities in all sorts of contexts, from driving ability to intelligence and moral character. So should we accept that self-deception is just our human lot?

Notice however that we've been talking about *moderate* self-delusion. I assume not many people would opt for the full-blown variety, like believing you're the queen, or that the CIA is after you. It's fair to think that this kind of delusion would lead to all sorts of negative consequences, and almost certainly get in the way of functioning properly and having a good life.

There is a large grey area between this and the moderate

self-deception that is supposed to be so advantageous. But the dangerous territory begins as soon as we stray from slight over-optimism to believing something in the face of contrary evidence. Perhaps there is a line to be drawn somewhere around there. But self-deception is insidious, and keeping it in check difficult. Even if it's true that a small amount of delusion comes bearing gifts, it could be argued that we should still endeavour to minimise it, and instead aim for the clear thinking that will help us to confront uncomfortable truths and take effective action.

But how is self-deception even possible? We don't have to think of self-deception as an exact parallel of interpersonal deception, with a mischievous inner being playing hide-and-seek. It may be more useful to see it as a kind of motivated, systematic mishandling of evidence. We so want to believe that s/he really loves us or we're the best candidate in the competition that we pay attention only to what confirms our preferred interpretation of reality, disregarding the evidence against it.

This can happen because we are a collection of many competing desires and inclinations. Perhaps there's a little voice in our head whispering, 'Are you sure about this?', but the voice in favour of adopting the ungrounded belief is louder and all but drowns the other one. So we end up bending and distorting the truth. In normal circumstances we'd be perfectly capable of seeing the facts in front of our eyes, but the motivation to believe misleads us into lowering our standards of evidence-sifting.

If self-deception is a kind of selective attention, we can guard against it at least to some degree by seeking to form a more objective picture of the situation and acquiring a habit of self-questioning. While pointing out the limits of introspection in his book *Incognito*, neuroscientist David Eagleman admits that 'we can learn to pay attention to what we're really seeing out there, as a painter does, and we can attend more closely to our internal signals, as a yogi does'.[63]

So in order to sharpen your inquiry you could test yourself by playing devil's advocate, for instance, or asking yourself what you would say to a friend in your situation, or what a good friend would say to you. Perhaps you could actually ask the good friend. It will never be possible to make our unconscious wholly conscious or be completely transparent to ourselves. The springs of action are normally shrouded in mist. But it's worth becoming more familiar with the intricacies of our mind so that we are at least a little less opaque.

The Sage

Self-deception is too familiar and recognisable a phenomenon for anyone to seriously doubt that it exists. But ask yourself how you deceive yourself, and you'll discover that you can do some things to yourself more easily than others.

Asking yourself a question is no more problematic than washing yourself, or teaching yourself. There is nothing paradoxical about adopting both roles of questioner and answerer, teacher and pupil. But how on earth can one be both the deceiver and the deceived? To do that you'd have to both know something and not know it at the same time, and you can hardly pull the wool over your own eyes without realising why it is you cannot see.

In many cases, you can get around the problem by reducing self-deception to a figure of speech and explaining what is going on in other terms. You are not hiding the truth from yourself if you simply don't go out and find it in the first place. For example, the talentless singer who auditions for a reality TV show is not deceiving himself about his abilities, he's simply unable to hear himself as others do, and not interested enough in trying to do so. Similarly, if you suspect that you have a terrible illness and you avoid going to a doctor, you are not hiding the truth from yourself, you're just refusing to look for it.

In many cases, however, we cannot seem to avoid the strange conclusion that people both know and don't know something at the same time. How is that possible? Because we all have many parts, and these parts do not all speak with one voice, or see the world in the same way. Common sense tells us that we each of us have a single mind that holds all our memories, beliefs and experiences. But neuroscience is increasingly confirming what many philosophers have thought for centuries: that this is an illusion. Our minds are a swirling mass of different impulses, capacities, thoughts and sensations that do not always link up neatly: the impulsive side of you might gobble up the cake you desire while your sensible side is distracted by something else.

Self-deception is puzzling only because we think of the self as a soloist when really each individual's mind is more like a jazz band, its different instruments playing their own lines. Usually they are in sufficient harmony for us to hear ourselves as a single piece of music. But every now and again, one member of the band will unilaterally pick up a different melodic line, and without realising it, we've played a completely different tune.

So we have at least two ways of thinking about apparent self-deception. In one there is no deception, simply a refusal or inability to attend to what we know or suspect will be uncomfortable truths. In the other, different facets of the self attend to different things and don't share the information. We could call these *inattention* and *divided attention* respectively, and only divided attention is what we'd usually call self-deception.

Could it be, however, as the recurrence of the word 'attention' suggests, that these are not two different phenomena at all, but two variants of the same one? That idea came to me as I was watching Alan Ayckbourn's play *Season's Greetings*. In the play, Neville and Belinda appear to have a lousy marriage. However, simply having a stable family life with a wife and children seems to suit Neville quite well, and he certainly doesn't want to jeopardise his comfortable situation just because relations with his wife are cool, to say the least. So what does he do when he has quite clear, but not conclusive evidence that Belinda has been, shall we say, cavorting with a house guest? He chooses to believe that they were both drunk and these things happen. And when the guest tries to tell him they weren't drunk at all, Neville simply tells him that they *were* drunk and if he says otherwise he'll kill him.

Is this self-deception? On the face of it, it looks like this is a straightforward example of inattention, a refusal to focus on inconvenient truths. But it didn't really work. The truth is too evident to be ignored completely, but too disturbing to be accepted as truth. So Neville had to quieten down the side of him that knew what really happened, allow himself to be distracted by other thoughts and so hope that the angry part of him would not be stirred to do something that the whole of him would regret. This seems better to fit the description of divided attention, which explains self-deception as involving different parts of the self competing for dominance. Yet no side emerges from this tussle completely victorious.

My suggestion is that Neville's case appears to fit neither model and both because really, there is only one: attention paid by the different parts of the self. If no part of the self pays much attention at all, we can avoid noticing uncomfortable truths in the first place. If only one part pays attention, others might be able to ignore it sufficiently for it to evade consciousness most of the time, but not always, and that is what appears to be self-deception. If one part is too insistent or all parts attend, we can't avoid the truth and we have ordinary conscious belief.

Neville's case occupies an interesting intermediate place in this taxonomy. He doesn't manage to drown out the plain and uncomfortable truth completely, so he seems too aware of what is going on to be fully self-deceived. But by refusing to pay further attention to the dalliance, it can in the normal run of things slip out of his consciousness, which is kept busy by other thoughts. He doesn't need to completely drown out the irritating voice of truth, he simply needs to make sure it's quiet enough that he can ignore it, which means, like background muzak, most of the time he doesn't notice it's there at all. He is not therefore self-deceived, merely *self-distracted*, which is simply a less potent version of the same thing. And if self-deception is common, surely self-distraction is even more ubiquitous.

Whether this particular suggestion is right or not, it is surely true that self-deception has to be explained in terms of the attentions of a divided self. Does this mean self-deception is inevitable? Up to a point, yes. We can never be entirely transparent to ourselves and so we can never know all the tricks our brains are playing on us. But by understanding better how these processes work, learning from past experience, and being suspicious of our own motives, we can learn to be more vigilant. The fatalism that says we can do nothing to counter self-deception is perhaps the most pernicious bit of self-deceit of them all.

THE STATUS OF STATUS

The Sage

—◦◦◦—

Over recent decades, evidence has piled up that human health and happiness are significantly affected by our place in the social hierarchy. Social epidemiologists such as Michael Marmot and the authors of *The Spirit Level*, Richard Wilkinson and Kate Pickett, have done the most to convert what was once a surprising theory into something now widely accepted as fact.[64]

What is normal or typical, however, is not always desirable or unchangeable. Any careful anthropological analysis would show that what confers status varies from place to place, and time to time. In many orthodox Jewish communities, for example, learning is more highly prized than wealth. Whereas four decades ago British teachers perceived their status to be 4.3 on a five-point scale, that figure has consistently been well under 3.0 for the last decade.[65] The idea that status matters has its own internal mutability. It is not simply a given of nature: it is something that we grant.

The way to deal with the 'fact' that status matters is not therefore simply to accept as inevitable the importance of our position on the economic league table. A better approach might be to try to challenge the assumptions we have about what should be valued. The most radical such challenge is to ask whether it would be desirable to try to do without it altogether. We probably can't eliminate it completely, but nor can we abolish murder, and that doesn't stop us doing our best to reduce it as much as possible.

There is a common line of thought that suggests status is morally objectionable, and so should be fought tooth and nail. The idea here is that all human lives are of equal worth, status raises some above others, and therefore status undermines our fundamental equality. Wherever you have high- and low-status individuals, you get inequality, where the interests and entitlements of the former are seen to trump those of the latter.

Against this it will be said that it would be crazy to totally eliminate status because, like it or not, we are not all equal in all respects. The high status of David Beckham and Nelson Mandela derives from a clear truth that both are exceptional in the fields of football and statesmanship respectively. The incongruous pairing is deliberate because it highlights the way to reconcile the egalitarian impulse with the proper recognition of exceptional expertise, talent or achievement. That is to say, status is fair and benign if conferred *locally*, in recognition of what makes someone stand out in a particular setting; but it's unjust and malign when conferred *globally*, raising some of the citizenry above others and treating them better whatever the context. The mismatch between the local and the global is most stark in aristocratic societies, where some people enjoy a higher status and greater privileges in almost every area of life despite being distinguished for an accident of birth that should not bring any status with it at all.

As a matter of fact, it seems that people tend to globalise some forms of status naturally, without thinking. The opinions of celebrities are listened to, even when they know no more than anyone else about the subject. They are given priority over others, for restaurant bookings and airline reservations. This is not inevitable. The over-endowment of status on celebrities is no more a universal, human phenomenon than the veneration of hereditary monarchs. As a society, we should try to move towards a situation in which people are praised for what makes them distinguished in their fields and treated just like anyone else outside of them. So, for instance, it's only right that David Beckham should have extremely high status as a footballer. But that does not mean he should be given special treatment in a court of law or that his views on politics should carry more weight than anyone else's.

Such a moderately meritocratic utopia seems a long way off, however. In the meantime, we could start by thinking about what we think should confer status. In some cases, it's quite simple: if you're a very good carpenter, you should have high status as a carpenter. But each kind of local status has its own status relative to the others. So, for example, we would value the world's best peace negotiator more than the world's best bingo caller. In addition to this, the local/global distinction I've already made is a little more complicated in the real world. There are some kinds of excellence that we take to justify respect that goes beyond the specific role in which the status emerged. Many of the qualities of statesmanship that gave Nelson Mandela his status as a political leader, for instance, also give us reasons to think of him as an exceptional human being. If you had a restaurant, you might well think that it would be right to cancel an ordinary customer's booking and give the table to him, and in most cases, even your customer would agree. So we need to think about the status of status: which varieties are most important and the extent to which they might deserve respect outside of the context in which they emerged.

Having at least got some clarity about how we see status, the most practical thing we can do is to make sure we live and work among people who regard it in ways similar to our own. For instance, if the idea of someone being treated better than others simply because they are rich appals you, then avoid joining clubs, associations or social circles where wealth is a status marker. Choose your peer group carefully, because in practice it's how they view status that affects us more directly than how that strange abstraction 'society as a whole' does. And if you find yourself looking down on those who give status to the wrong people, remember that by doing so, you're playing the same ranking game. The question with status is how, not if, to confer it.

The Shrink

Behind much human activity is the drive to seek fame and fortune – or even just shift up the pecking order a little. It began deep in our evolutionary history. We strive for status just like male chimps broadcast their dominance by slapping their hands, stamping their feet, and noisily dragging branches. Just like them, we want to be a 'big noise'. But we fail to notice the similarities, and our own behaviour seems to us of a completely different order.

With us, that drive shows itself in things like compulsively comparing ourselves to others, a competitive spirit, aiming to get to the top of one's profession, an ambition to acquire wealth or power or climb social ladders, a desire to be respected and recognised. What's wrong with that, you may ask. These aims are natural and endorsed by the society we live in, which encourages competition and self-evaluation based on external markers of social status.

One problem with status is that it often gets too mixed up with achievement, which does seem to be a valuable piece of the mental health jigsaw. In the short term, achieving something tends to make us feel good. Accomplishment finds its way into Martin Seligman's top five components of well-being because it's something that people consistently pursue for its own sake.[66] Without a belief in our ability to attain our goals – self-efficacy, in psychological jargon – we are likely to lead a restricted, stunted life.

But even the most successful life can be blighted by a nagging sense that one does not quite measure up, feelings of failure and underachievement, obsessing about what our peers have achieved that we haven't. Seeing the world as made up of winners and losers and counting ourselves among the latter doesn't do much for our sense of well-being.

It's common to fancy that the solution lies in raising our status by achieving more: a better job, house, body would halt the gnawing dissatisfaction and fill us with lasting feelings of contentment. But it doesn't work that way. This strategy risks becoming a race we can never win. There will always be people who in our eyes have achieved more than us, and we could constantly be running to try to catch up with them. Along this road of judging ourselves in comparison to others await stress, anxiety and depression.

However, a steadfast rejection of the pursuit of status can be difficult in a culture that privileges it. Critical self-judgements based on social rank can slip into our psyche unnoticed even when we have consciously rejected those values. And there's always the suspicion that our avowed dismissal of hierarchies we have failed to ascend is just a case of sour grapes.

Of course religious traditions the world over have long been wary of such shallow, worldly, material goals, and preached getting away from them in favour of a deeper connection with ourselves, the world and others. Renowned primatologist Frans de Waal reports that in the thirteenth century Saint Bonaventura pronounced that: 'The higher a monkey climbs, the more you see of its behind.'[67]

It's not only religions that have warned us against devoting our lives to the pursuit of status. For the Stoics, this would be an example of something that is not in our control and therefore not to be valued. Aristotle acknowledged that things like money and recognition don't count for nothing, but what they count for is limited. Money is after all only a means to an end. And recognition matters only if it's well deserved, and if we are being praised by people we respect. (See also the section on Aristotle.) For these philosophers, what really matters is following reason and improving our moral character.

We don't all have to renounce the world in favour of the contemplative life (although some of us might want to). But we are left with a question, which is to what extent we ought to endorse our innate craving for status. We are mammals, so we know that intimations of high status will probably make us feel good. But just because this drive happens to be part of our evolved toolkit, it doesn't mean we must mindlessly acquiesce to it. It would be very easy to tell ourselves there's nothing we can do about it, and justify any behaviour by saying: 'We're primates; that's what primates do.'

Instead, we could just recognise the little *frisson* that status sends through our body and decide not to follow where it leads. According to psychologist Paul Gilbert: 'The desire for sex, fame, fortune and the nice things of life are millions of years old – they work through us; it is up to us, though, if we want to run mindlessly down the road after them.'[68] We could question, challenge conventional views, clarify what success really means to us. We could use our capacity for reflection to decide for ourselves what is truly worth doing and what actually gives meaning to our life.

Life does not have to be a race, and competition should be balanced by other things. Bertrand Russell wrote that 'success can only be one ingredient in happiness, and is too dearly purchased if all the other ingredients have been sacrificed to obtain it'.[69] It's worth giving some thought to what we're losing when we focus so much on winning, as well as what we're gaining.

I have found two perspectives on this particularly useful. One is Paul Gilbert's distinction between *threat-based* and *value-based* achievement striving.[70] We should endeavour to do things because we value them, not in order to escape feelings of anxiety about our place on the social ladder. The other comes from Acceptance and Commitment Therapy: in Russ Harris's words, 'success is living by our values'.[71]

Even if a certain amount of comparison is natural and unavoidable, we can create more balance by paying attention to what we are content with, savouring small things, engaging in activities we enjoy for their own sake, and seeking non-competitive social interactions. We don't have to banish status from the good life, but we should put it in its proper place.

ARE YOU RESPONSIBLE?

The Sage

~~~~~

Like 'wealthy tycoon' or 'thin ballerina', the adjective in 'responsible adult' can usually be taken for granted. In ordinary circumstance, to be an adult just is to be someone who is responsible for your actions. Nor is the everyday concept of responsibility an obscure one: you are responsible for anything that happens as a consequence of something you had control over and that you could reasonably be expected to have anticipated. This holds whatever the consequence of what we do or neglect to do. We are as responsible for failing to look after a very young child as we are for mistreating one, as much to blame for letting someone drive off in a car with brakes we know are faulty as we are for fitting broken ones.

Of course, the issue becomes much more complicated when you get bogged down in the seemingly interminable and intractable philosophical debate over free will. But these metaphysical difficulties have surprisingly little impact on real life. No matter how persuaded a philosopher might be that free will is an illusion, she will bring up her children to have a sense of responsibility and will react very differently to someone who unwittingly serves an off piece of meat from one who knowingly poisons a kebab.

The real-world complications of responsibility arise more from psychological than metaphysical factors. In principle, it seems very clear that responsibility should be proportionate to the degree of control one has over consequences. In practice, however, we attribute praise and blame very differently to situations in which exactly the same degree of control is in place and the consequences are very similar. For instance, you would be judged morally culpable if you didn't walk across a shallow stream to try to save one child at the cost of your £70 shoes, but few would think you reprehensible for not putting £50 in a collection tin to almost certainly save ten lives, even though it's cheaper and easier. There may be less certainty about the outcome, but even an action that has a 50/50 chance of saving several lives is at least as demanding of our time as something that is very likely to save one. Yet hardly anyone thinks that not giving enough to charity is anywhere near as blameworthy as passing by while a young child drowns.

So what makes the difference? The answer appears to be simply geographical proximity. It seems that the more direct the physical contact between agent and consequence, the more we feel people are responsible. This has been suggested most starkly by a whole set of experiments around people's willingness to sacrifice the life of one person in order to save many more. People have been asked for their responses to a large set of variations on the 'trolley problem' (previously mentioned in 'Gut feelings and instincts'), a thought experiment in which people can stop a runaway train ploughing into a group of people by, variously, diverting the train onto another track where fewer will die, pushing a fat man onto the line and blocking the train, pulling a lever and dropping the man onto the line through a trap door, and so on and so on. With the benefit of fMRI scans, experimenters seem to have shown that the differences in people's willingness to act are based more on emotion than principle. It just feels wrong to push a man to his death, whereas it doesn't feel wrong to pull a switch that leads to even more people dying.

This obviously has troubling consequences for things like modern warfare where fighting can be done by remote control, making it easier for soldiers to kill. But it also has implications closer to home for most of us. In any area of life where issues of responsibility arise, it seems likely that we are not going to attribute praise and blame according to how much control people really have, but on the basis of emotional factors concerning physical contact that are arguably morally irrelevant. So, downloading an illegal copy of a film feels less wrong than buying a pirated DVD from a dodgy-looking guy in a market; largely ignoring the plight of sick children in Angola feels much less wrong than being mean in the whip-round in the pub for the local kid with leukaemia; reading your partner's emails feels less sneaky than reading their written diary; eating cheap chicken nuggets feels fine, just as long as we don't have to see the factory farm the bird is bred in, and so on.

Is it possible to be sanguine about these apparent inconsistencies? There are sometimes reasons for being less worried about such cases than rational moral philosophers suggest we should be. The fact that our moral sense is tied in with feelings of empathy is not just a good thing, it is arguably what allows morality to get off the ground in the first place. But even if the emotional triggers for a sense of responsibility are in general a good thing, that doesn't mean we should just allow them to lead us astray.

On the other hand, there are surely limits as to what we can do about this. No matter how intellectually convinced we might become that we have a duty, for instance, to make sure what we buy from the developing world is ethically sourced, we just can't sustain the feeling that this is vitally important 24/7.

But the impossibility of a decisive victory against the forces of irrationality should not be reason to give up trying to control them altogether, if the need to do so is a moral one. And there is a simple rule of thumb that can help us here: if we are thinking about how responsible we are for actions, we need to be aware of the extent to which physical proximity makes a difference and do what we can, however imperfectly, to factor that in. Responsibility is then one of many areas in life where philosophy and psychology leave us with the message: Do not trust your feelings. We carry responsibility for whatever is within our control, whether we feel its weight or not.

The Shrink

◦◦◦

Of all the quotidian issues constantly testing our wisdom, how much responsibility to take for things is one of the hardest to get right, or even think clearly about. Both taking too much and too little responsibility are common, and staples of therapy sessions.

We all know what too little looks like. Many people seem to lack any kind of responsibility reflex, reaching for the blame button without second thought any time something goes wrong: it's the fault of others, the past, the government, everything under the sun. Indeed, in some therapies the appearance of any flicker of responsibility would be seen as a very significant turn of events. If we can see that we are not just passive recipients but have a role in directing the play of our life, we may be able to take action to turn things around.

You may think that the risk of being too responsible is slight, that the more the merrier in this context. But an excess of responsibility can be just as much of a problem. The symptoms include beliefs to the effect that you hold the key to your own and other people's well-being, that if anything goes wrong it's down to you, that whatever befalls you is the product of your free choices, and if it turns out to be unsatisfactory you'll be to blame for not making different ones. Quite a burden to carry through life.

Not surprisingly, thinking that everything that goes wrong is your fault comes with corrosive feelings of guilt and the perception that you have done something wrong whether you have or not. Of course guilt can be an appropriate response. If you've acted badly, feelings of guilt will alert you to the fact that you'd better do something about it and get on with making amends – although it's worth remembering that wallowing in self-loathing won't help. But once we acquire the guilt habit it can be hard to tell whether what we're feeling guilty about is or isn't within our control.

We can properly hold ourselves responsible only if something was in fact in our power. Of course I'm talking about common-or-garden responsibility, and I won't even begin to discuss the different and metaphysical point that *ultimately* nobody has any, since that thought does not usually help to deal with daily life.

Excesses of responsibility can be tricky to spot. It should be clear that if you hit someone it's appropriate to take responsibility for the action, unless you are drugged, ill, under the influence of hypnotic suggestion, or afflicted by some such condition. You might try to avoid blame by claiming you were provoked, but even if you were justified you should still take responsibility. If, on the other hand, it rains every day of what you hoped would be the perfect holiday with your spouse, it should be equally clear that it couldn't be your fault. But if you try hard enough you might still manage to blame yourself.

What makes this particularly difficult to think about is that it's easy to assume that if we at least partly cause something to happen we must be somehow culpable. If our holidaymaker was of the self-blaming kind, for instance, he could easily blame himself for the rain because it was only to suit him that they went away that week rather than the following, sunny, one. More seriously, I suspect most people would feel guilty if they had encouraged someone to take a train rather than drive and the train had crashed, even though they could never have foreseen that.

But even when we have contributed to an outcome to some degree, we should make sure that the amount of responsibility we take is proportionate. A useful Cognitive-Behaviour Therapy tool for this kind of situation is the responsibility pie. If you are feeling bad about something and suspect you might be taking too much onto yourself, list all the people and circumstances that contributed to a certain outcome, then draw a pie chart, allocating bigger or smaller slices depending on your judgement of relative responsibility. Christine Padesky suggests drawing your own slice at the end so you are not tempted to assign yourself too much prematurely.[72] Of course mathematical precision is not the aim. We can't disentangle all the complex interactions that led to a situation. The main object of the exercise is to see that there are many factors contributing to any outcome and try to tease out the major ones.

The tension between attributing too much and too little responsibility also turns up in our relationships with others. People are to some extent the product of their circumstances, and taking context into account is laudable: 'She had a hard life'; 'He was brought up like that'. Remembering this can help us to have more compassion towards them. But a relationship is a system, and our own actions affect the way it develops. If we excuse too much we risk creating an environment in which the other person is not encouraged to take responsibility. It may be true that she had a hard life, but that doesn't mean she is forever justified in not making an effort. A particularly unfortunate combination is when one partner has a tendency to take on too much responsibility and the other too little.

We have to hold people responsible unless we have good reason not to, like in the case of the man whose sudden paedophilic urges turned out to be caused by a brain tumour. And we have to hold ourselves responsible for the broad direction of our life, trying to avoid both delusions of grandeur and reducing ourselves to helpless victims. We should put our actions in their proper perspective and aim at a fair assessment of responsibility all round.

The line between remembering that things happen in contexts and justifying or excusing may be thin but it's hugely important. We should watch out that we don't let mitigation turn into exculpation.

THE HAPPY PESSIMIST

The Shrink

———∞———

Among Seneca's most insistent advice was that of getting into the habit of imagining that the worst was not only possible but imminent: 'an hour, an instant of time, suffices for the overthrow of empires. ... This is why we need to envisage every possibility and to strengthen the spirit to deal with the things which may conceivably come about. Rehearse them in your mind: exile, torture, war, shipwreck.'[73] And, in a nutshell: 'Just where death is expecting you is something we cannot know; so, for your part, expect him everywhere.'[74]

I wonder what Rhonda Byrne, author of bestseller self-help book *The Secret*, would make of this. So different is her advice, based on what is usually known as 'the law of attraction', that it seems to emanate from a parallel universe. The basic idea is that like attracts like: if you believe that things like wealth and success will come your way, they will. This is positive thinking at its most extreme. It's not just that by having positive thoughts you are more likely to behave in ways that produce positive outcomes, which would be more or less sensible. No, it's the thoughts themselves that, magically, attract these outcomes.

This, if you managed to get yourself to believe it, would be very soothing. But Seneca's advice also has an oddly comforting effect. Both recur in self-help literature. But both can't be true. So which shall we adopt as a life-guiding principle? This could make a difference to how we manage our mental life from day to day.

Optimism has found a more sensible advocate in positive psychology, which has suggested that optimists have superior health outcomes, longer life expectancy and generally do better than their pessimistic counterparts. However, these results are not wholly uncontroversial.[75]

On the other hand, some findings suggest that people who are mildly depressed have more accurate perceptions of reality. Far from negative appraisals being a mist engulfing clear thinking, it is non-depressed thinking that may be a kind of self-deluded fog shielding us from what we don't want to see. Perceiving things clearly is valuable in helping us to take appropriate action. A rose-tinted optimism is shallow and unrealistic, and might ultimately do us a disservice.

There seem to be enough doubts to wonder whether, instead of closing our eyes and making a wish, it may be beneficial to anticipate what can go wrong and prepare for it. Julie Norem, author of *Defensive Pessimism*, reckons that this can be a useful strategy for people who are anxious about the future. We're not talking about embracing worrying with abandon, however: this is about thinking about possible scenarios in detail and making contingency plans.

On the side of gloom is not only Hank Williams, who sang that 'No matter how I struggle and strive, / I'll never get out of this world alive', but the Buddha himself, whose very first noble truth is that life is suffering. There is no getting away from this – shit does happen, we lose what we love and painful things inevitably come our way. Even the most charmed life cannot escape old age and death, and with it the end of life's delights.

So should we bother with optimism? It does partly depend on what we mean by optimism. Even in the positive psychology literature, different understandings of this pop up in different places. For instance, optimism is sometimes equated not with holding positive beliefs about the future, but with resilience, the ability to adjust and spring back after setbacks. Now, this really is a quality worth having.

The ideal would be to balance the awareness that bad things may happen with lashings of appreciation and resilience. These are the qualities that will help us to make the most of whatever circumstances we find ourselves in, and bounce back when things do go wrong. But adding a pinch of pessimism could make our appreciation even deeper. So from the Stoics we can take away a reminder of the fragility of life, and from positive psychology the importance of gratitude and resilience.

A good approach is what Viktor Frankl, author of *Man's Search for Meaning*, called 'tragic optimism', referring to the ability to make the best of any situation in the face of the 'tragic triad' of pain, guilt and death. He believed it was possible to say 'yes to life in spite of everything' by '(1) turning suffering into a human achievement and accomplishment;

(2) deriving from guilt the opportunity to change oneself for the better; and (3) deriving from life's transitoriness an incentive to take responsible action.'[76]

A softening of our beliefs about the future could also help. Positive and negative outcomes unstably morph into each other, and we never really know how things will eventually turn out. Since nothing about the future is certain at all, neither a strong belief that things are bound to be great nor a conviction that they will be awful is justified.

We have no reason not to be happy pessimists, suspending judgement about the future and cherishing whatever life has to offer in full knowledge of its impermanence. In short, we should count our blessings but not our chickens.

The Sage

In the world of arts and ideas, those who are hailed as prophets of the age usually talk of decline, disaster or the dark night of the soul. Think of Kierkegaard's *Fear and Trembling*, Sartre's *Nausea*, or Conrad's *Heart of Darkness*. You don't gain a reputation for depth by saying that the world isn't all that bad really and starting a sing-song.

When it comes to politics, however, our heroes are those who focus on the next dawn, not the imminent dusk.

Barack Obama talked of the audacity of hope, not its futility; Martin Luther King had a dream, not a nightmare.

Perhaps this is a natural result of an intellectual division of labour. As honest and insightful observers of the human condition, intellectuals must be able to see all that is rotten in the world. Good leaders, in contrast, need to have a positive vision of what we can do about it. Ideally, both sets of considerations would coexist in the same mind. Grim diagnoses are futile if they are not accompanied by effective prescriptions, and inspirational leadership is empty if it ignores inconvenient truths.

The problem with intellectual doomsayers, however, is that their pessimism is indiscriminate. And as Matt Ridley argues in *The Rational Optimist*, the dire predictions of past pessimists haven't got a good record for accuracy.[77] So perhaps our tendency to equate darkness with depth is as irrational as a Panglossian optimism. What we often praise as a profound ability to see in the dark is often no more than an inability or unwillingness to turn on the light.

What then happens when we do turn on that light? It's tempting to say that a rational, objective view has no time for optimism or pessimism, just realism. The question is not whether the glass is half-full or half-empty, but exactly how much of what kind of liquid it contains. But this won't do. A viewpoint that assigns no value is no viewpoint at all, it's merely an inventory or a map. Making sense of the world requires us to go beyond assembling the brute facts and judging what matters about them. It's in this gap between the facts and what we make of them that the opportunity for taking either a rosy or bleak view emerges.

For me, the profoundest example of this comes in the difference between French existentialism and its British counterpart: Pythonism. Jean-Paul Sartre, Albert Camus and Monty Python essentially take the same view of the absurdity and meaninglessness of life. The difference is that, whereas Sartre described the response to this as involving anguish, abandonment and despair, the Pythons just laughed. As has often been remarked, the difference between comedy and tragedy can often be no more than one of perspective: given enough time or distance, what seems terrible can look comically absurd. Nothing expresses the fine line between the two better than the simple couplet in 'Always Look on the Bright Side of Life', sung in *Life of Brian* by the crucified as they hang dying on their crosses: 'Life's a piece of shit / When you look at it.' Semantically, this is as bleak a view of life as you can imagine. But with the rhyme and the jaunty melody, it's transformed into bathos.

This is not to say that the facts aren't important. Positive or negative responses can be more or less appropriate and the role of hard-headed realism is to ensure that we are actually responding to how things really are, not just as we perceive them to be. Whether it's appropriate to whistle while you die may be a matter of opinion, but there would be something terribly wrong about cheerfully singing because you falsely thought you weren't going to die at

all, or to succumb to despair if your condition wasn't ter-
minal. So although the facts need not determine our complete response to them, they do place limits on the range of
responses that is appropriate. Whether we don rose-tinted
spectacles or dark shades should depend on what the
natural light is like.

Even here, though, I'm not sure the distinction between
optimism and pessimism is the key one. In assessing how
good or bad things are now, we certainly need realism, but
surely the same is true of any assessment about how things
are likely to be down the line. So the difference I have identified between Sartre and Python is actually nothing to
do with judgement but attitude. That's why the common
metaphor of the glass half-full or half-empty is misleading. For sure, it's important how we frame things, so using
positive or negative words colours our perception in ways
that might distort it. But what really matters is whether
we make the best or the worst of whatever it is we've got,
not how we describe it. So it's better, for instance, to see
a half-empty cup as containing enough water to quench
your thirst than seeing a half-full one as not worth drinking. Indeed, it is surely sometimes more helpful to think
on the basis of making the most of what is imperfect than
trying to kid yourself that what we have to work on is more
ideal than it really is. To make good choices we need to
detect threats and limitations as well as opportunities.

Looked at in this way, optimism and pessimism appear
to drop out of the picture. When it comes to seeing things

how they are, what's needed is realism. When it comes to deciding what to do about it, a positive attitude may help, but that is not the same as having a belief that things will be OK, which is what optimism about the future suggests.

But perhaps the biggest problem with thinking about our outlook in terms of optimism and pessimism is that there simply is no global policy about which is better. If you ask me whether I'm an optimist or a pessimist, I really can't say. On the one hand, I think there is an unbearable amount of pointless suffering in the world, miserable lives that will never be redeemed. I believe that the contentment and good fortune I enjoy right now will pass, and that the chances are before I die, many of the things and people I most value will suffer or perish. On the other, I would say I'm more cheerful than not and that there are many wonderful things in the world, and the older I get, the more they seem to be found in a tiny number of people and small, everyday things like a home-baked loaf of bread, or the sight of a robin feeding in the garden. The world can look amazing or dreadful, depending on the perspective you take, and I do not always take the same one. Perhaps then realism should be seen as not a single, neutral view, but the ability to take multiple viewpoints and to take them all into account, neglecting neither those that expose the flaws nor those that bring out the beauty. Neither a pessimist nor an optimist be. Be both.

NO REGRETS?

The Sage

—◦⟨⦾⟩◦—

When it comes to regret, most people seem to think that Frank Sinatra got it right: it's OK to have a few, as long as they are too few to mention. Regretting too much is a far greater risk than regretting too little.

However, there seems to be something of a double standard at work here, for when we look at people in public life, few things seem to raise the hackles more than lack of regret. The biggest gaffe of Norman Lamont's political career came when the then Chancellor of the Exchequer said: '*Je ne regrette rien.*' Three weeks later, he was out of a job. And ever since Tony Blair left office, many people have been waiting for him to express some remorse for sending British troops to Iraq, and each missed opportunity to do so has led to more damning words against him.

What explains this demand for regret in others and reluctance to regret ourselves? The answer could be that mistakes come in two varieties: prudential and moral. Prudential mistakes – from buying the wrong food blender to missing a once-in-a-lifetime opportunity – may show poor judgement, but they do not cast doubt on our good character.

Failing to keep a promise or betraying a confidence,

in contrast, are usually moral failings. They stand on the record as testimony of our failure to do the right thing. To regret these mistakes is to look back at our actions and admit to ourselves that if we had been better people, we would not have done them. This is no more than moral honesty requires.

Rather conveniently, however, we are apt to see the mistakes of others as moral, and our own as purely prudential – or not mistakes at all. You fail to keep a promise and you're a cad; I fail to keep one and it was because of a lapse of memory or an unavoidable conflict. You cheat on your spouse and you're a rotten bastard; I have an affair and it was a natural response to feelings of rejection at home and uncontrollable passion at the office. We rightly see that others should acknowledge their moral shortcomings but fail to be as morally demanding of ourselves.

But why should anyone dwell on the past at all? What is done is done, people often say, just water under the bridge. No use worrying about what you can't change. But that's too simplistic. First of all, there is often a great deal that you can and should change in the light of regret. Most obviously, many wrongs can be put right, or at least tidied up so they are not such a huge mess. And often showing regret is the prerequisite for this. If you ruin a friendship, for example, healing it usually requires that you express some remorse for your actions.

But the kind of change that regret can inspire is not just directed to putting things right. Regret can make us think about how we will behave in the future, so as to avoid making the same mistakes again. George Santayana's famous quote, 'Those who cannot remember the past are condemned to repeat it', is most commonly invoked in relation to politics and history but is arguably even more pertinent when applied to the individual.

There is a second reason why an inability to alter the past should not eliminate regret. The mere fact that you cannot change what has happened does not mean you are not responsible for it. Indeed, we often hold people most severely to account for things that are irreversible, such as the destruction of a work of art, an important cultural artefact or a human life. Having a sense of responsibility is vital to our moral sense. Without it we become indifferent to the bad consequences of our actions, thoughtless, callous, selfish and insensitive. If you are to take responsibility for your actions, you do so whether they can be undone or not. Living with bad feelings about things you cannot change is thus a price we pay for being fully moral creatures. Feeling responsible only for things we can change is not just practically impossible, it diminishes what responsibility means.

That is not to say that all regret is good, of course. It comes in better and worse forms. The best provoke remedial action, reform of character or the deepening of moral wisdom. The worst become a kind of indulgent wallowing in miserable thought which neither puts things right nor improves ourselves.

Regret can also reflect an inability to deal with the imperfections of life and ourselves. When we kick ourselves because we should have been able to make a better decision, the root of our mistake is not just that hindsight is always 20/20. All decisions are made on the basis of limited information, and the lack of knowledge about what will happen next is only a small part of that data deficit. The fundamental problem is not to do with where we stand in time, but how much of it we have. We just don't have enough to think through every implication of every choice, gather all the facts that relate to it, or even do the research to find out which sorts of facts are most crucial. Inevitably, when we do come to choose, we will therefore do so on the basis of information that is not only partial but probably does not include the right balance of the important and the incidental. To try too hard to overcome this, to always seek as much information and weigh up as many arguments as you can, would be the kind of obsessive compulsive behaviour that would interfere with your ability to get on and live. And so, inevitably, almost every decision you have ever made is sub-optimal if you think about it enough – or perhaps I should say too much. Regrets are misguided when they are rooted in this kind of retrospective perfectionism, an excessive desire to interrogate the wisdom of past choices so much that eventually failings are bound to be exposed.

The problem with regret is therefore not always that we have too much of it, but that we often have too much of the wrong kind. We should be suspicious of people who say they regret *rien*, even if that person is you. If we think we have too few regrets to mention, then perhaps that's just because there are some mistakes we won't even admit to ourselves.

There is one more reason to at least accept our regrets, even if we don't eliminate them. In the Ray Bradbury short story 'A Sound of Thunder', the whole of human history is changed by one time traveller treading on a single butterfly.[78] Our own small lives can also turn on apparently small events: a missed bus leads to a chance encounter; a job application lands on the desk of a recruiter made crabby by pre-lunch hunger, not an hour earlier when she was cheerfully drinking mid-morning coffee. So even if we do regret some of the things we have done, we should accept that even a small difference in the past might have changed the direction our lives have taken. If we want to embrace what we have today we have to accept what we did yesterday.

The Shrink

Recently I came across the saying that when you argue with reality you lose 100 per cent of the time. Very apt, I thought. It could be helpful in dealing with consuming regret, the kind that really eats you up.

And regret does eat us up. Our minds tirelessly spin mesmerising stories about the terrible mistakes we've made and clearly superior alternatives we've let slip past. We keep going over the events in our minds as if it were just possible that at some crucial point the action would shift to a parallel world and yield a different outcome. These mental machinations can last months, even years, all the time preventing us from noticing the world around us and telling us that if only we'd done the other thing …

It's a very human feeling, regret, relying as it does on imagining and evaluating different scenarios and feeling responsible for choosing the wrong one. It can be really hard to let go of what we think might have been. We are often wholly aware that wallowing in regret doesn't help, that no matter how much we obsess about it the past will not change, that instead of filling our head with 'what ifs' we could be enjoying what we have now. But those soothing lines that friends come up with – 'the past is the past', 'it's done now', or 'it was meant to be' – don't always do the job.

Regrets come in different grades. There are the short-term ones about buying the wrong blow-drier, or choosing the wrong holiday. As Barry Schwartz explains in *The Paradox of Choice*, this kind of regret finds fertile ground in an environment that constantly throws options at us. Then it's easy to be dissatisfied with our choice even if in fact there isn't much wrong with it, and imagine that a different one would have been better. The more options we have the more likely it is we'll regret our choice. The antidote, according to Schwartz, is to go for good enough rather than perfect, and cultivate gratitude for what we do have.

It may be true that a choice we made was not optimal. But where does it say we must choose perfectly at all times? And how much does it really matter anyway? (Of course there may be some unforeseeable way in which it will turn out to matter, for better or for worse, but we can't factor in the unforeseeable.) We could ask ourselves, is this a regret we're likely to take to our grave? A negative answer may not erase the feeling at one stroke, but it should draw attention to the fact that time will likely take care of it. It will pass.

Then there are the more serious regrets, the ones we do take to our graves. And there are many of these, about both doing and not doing: marrying the wrong person, choosing the wrong career, being nasty to a friend, not spending enough time with our family, not taking more risks, not having children, not travelling around the world, not developing a talent.

These are hard to shrug off. And indeed there would be something wrong about shrugging them off. It's right and proper to regret hurting people or otherwise acting badly, and advisable to reflect deeply on our big existential choices at times. A militantly unregretting attitude can slide into unwillingness to take responsibility for our actions or learn from our mistakes.

We can use regret constructively by taking it as a starting point for self-examination. For instance, we could ask ourselves what the regret tells us about our values and whether we can do something to bring our actions more into line. If we think we should have travelled more or spent more time with our family, can we still do so? If we hurt someone, how can we make amends?

It's also worth reflecting on the conditions leading to our choice. We often convince ourselves we should have known better. But is that true? Could our past self really have known better? Are we taking circumstances into account? If we do think we had the knowledge to make a better choice, what contributed to making it inoperative? In any case, what can we learn from this that might help us to make wiser choices in the future?

And let's not forget that in many cases our choice brought us gains as well as losses. We might want to turn our attention to the benefits of the life choices we did make. But then we must do this carefully. Human beings are biased towards justifying the decisions they did make, which can lead to self-deception. We don't want to convince ourselves that there were no losses when there were. Only if we acknowledge both sides will we be able to take corrective action.

For instance, I once gave myself months of regret after moving away from a flat I loved. Through lengthy soul-searching I realised that one of the mistakes I'd made was to allow my hard-to-pin-down uncomfortable feelings about selling up to be silenced by the good reasons for it. This is not to say that impalpable hunches should always trump other reasons, but I should at least have given them a good airing. I was also wrong to feel, once the process had started, that an unstoppable juggernaut had been set into motion and there was nothing I could do about it. These learning points came in handy in future decisions.

But a more profound tack in combating regret is that we can never know how things would have worked out if we'd taken another path, so often we just can't be sure that the choice we made was in fact wrong. As Milan Kundera reminds us in *The Unbearable Lightness of Being*, 'living only one life, we can neither compare it with our previous lives nor perfect it in our lives to come'.[79] Our regret is only a snapshot at one point in time. From our current point of view it may seem obvious that we made the wrong choice, but our future perspective may be quite different. A setback can lead to new opportunities, success to future heartache.

There is a Chinese story that illustrates this perfectly:

There is an old farmer in a poor country village who is considered well-off because he owns a horse. One day the horse runs away. The neighbours sympathise, saying how terrible this is, but the farmer simply replies 'maybe'. A few days later the horse returns, bringing with it some wild horses. The neighbours rejoice, but the farmer simply says 'maybe'. The next day the farmer's son tries to ride one of the wild horses, but is thrown and breaks his leg. When the neighbours come to offer their sympathy, again the farmer just says 'maybe'. The following week military officials come to the village to draft young men into the army, but the farmer's son is rejected because of his broken leg. The neighbours congratulate the farmer, but he replies 'maybe' ...

We can never entirely banish regret: it comes with the human condition. But whenever we find ourselves thinking of what might have been we could remind ourselves of the farmer's maybe.

MEANING AND SPIRITUALITY

The Shrink

❧

The route to meaning can be tortuous. There are times in life when we experience a sense of emptiness, an inner lack, a feeling that some mysterious vital ingredient has gone missing from our life. You kind of know what you … *mean* when you find yourself thinking, or hear other people saying, that life has lost its meaning, but if you try to capture it the whole thing dissolves into a puff of air, leaving you puzzled about how to get it back. The way to meaning can be as evanescent as its definition.

Sometimes we interpret this kind of experience as a spiritual yearning, perhaps connected with a wavering of religious belief, which leads us to seek places like churches and retreat centres, searching for God or some other connection with the transcendent. This may well provide just what some people are looking for, endowing them with a renewed sense of purpose.

But although a spiritual yearning is a common accompaniment to being human, the religious temperament can become separated from the belief. Many of us continue to crave some form of spirituality long after the belief has gone. At those times, are we forced to choose between either going along with a religion whose dogmas have become unacceptable or ignoring a vacuum somewhere near the centre of our being?

In the fluid times we live in, the spiritual can be interestingly redefined to suit our purposes. For a while I have been noticing spas and beauty salons that call themselves Zen something, or feature statues of the Buddha in their glossy brochures. Being spiritual used to mean things like getting up at three o'clock in the morning, self-denial, mortification of the flesh. Now spirituality and hedonism seem to be sliding ever closer. Since we are embodied creatures, a softening of the boundaries between the material and the spiritual seems appropriate. But ultimately this blurring may not work, since it risks robbing the spiritual of anything distinctive and reducing it to a feel-good experience.

We may have to accept that no matter how intense our yearnings, some of what we crave may be unattainable. If we're genuinely seeking the divine, the eternal, brahman, we may or may not be able to find it. But there may be other ways of responding to our desire to live a life that goes beyond the purely materialistic.

Sometimes meaning is linked with the broader concept of transcendence rather than that of spirituality. Martin Seligman, for instance, defines meaning as 'belonging to and serving something that you believe is bigger than the self'.[80] While this definition lends itself to a religious interpretation, it can clearly include things like political or humanitarian work, say, as well as taking part in a spiritual practice. But many people just don't feel this connection with something bigger, religious or otherwise. Must they accept that their lives are meaningless?

If spirituality or transcendence were strictly necessary to find meaning, those of a more naturalistic bent would be condemned to a meaningless life. But meaning can and does arise from the world around us, often in ways that are too small to notice. On the other hand, perhaps we shouldn't be too quick to dismiss transcendence: in one of its guises, it might play a role in the creation of meaning after all.

As well as being a psychiatrist and concentration camp survivor, Viktor Frankl was the author of *Man's Search for Meaning* and founder of *logotherapy*, which he described as a 'meaning-centred psychotherapy'. In his writings he addressed our innate orientation towards meaning and the 'existential vacuum' that can sometimes engulf us. But this void is not to be overcome by looking inward, since a narrow concern for our own state of mind is not conducive to a meaningful life. We can more readily find meaning when we engage with things outside ourselves. Although Frankl was a religious man himself, this kind of transcendence doesn't seem to require a spiritual realm or anything *bigger* than oneself. It simply requires a focus on things *other* than ourselves. Perhaps this is the most useful kind.

In Frankl's words, life 'can be made meaningful (1) by what we give to the world in terms of our creation; (2) by what we take from the world in terms of our experience; and (3) by the stand we take toward the world, that is to say, by the attitude we choose toward suffering'.[81]

The last is perhaps the most difficult. According to Frankl, it's possible to find meaning even when we are faced with a hopeless situation. However constrained our circumstances, we always have the last freedom of choosing how to respond. At Auschwitz, he had a good chance to practise this lesson. But Frankl thought that suffering was not *necessary* to find meaning, and that if it's open to us to change the situation for the better that's what we should do.

So we can find meaning through *creation* – getting involved with a project, 'creating a work or doing a deed';[82] *experience* – encountering someone or something, be it nature, art, or loving another human being; and *attitude* – choosing the way we respond to events and circumstances. Adopting one or any combination of these paths can be enough to breathe meaning back into life.

The Sage

For philosophers, loss of meaning in life is an occupational hazard. It happened in Germany in the late nineteenth century, when Friedrich Nietzsche wrote of the nihilism that confronts us once the claims of religion and objective truth have been shown to be false. It happened in Britain in 1936, when A.J. Ayer's *Language, Truth and Logic* heralded the arrival of logical positivism, with its belief that statements about life's meaning were literally meaningless. And it happened in France in the 1940s, when the existentialists Camus and Sartre announced that life had no pre-existing purpose.

But these philosophers did not so much deny meaning as redefine it. The meaning of life does not exist as a fact in the world, waiting to be discovered. We are not born with a purpose, but that does not mean we have to live without purpose. There is no meaning *of* life, but there can be meaning *in* life, if we put it there ourselves. And the place to put it is not in the mindless reasons for our past creation or a future purpose that just isn't there, but in a form of living that is meaningful in and of itself. What we call a meaningful life is simply a life worth living, one in which existence has a value not for what it might lead to, but for what it is.

But how do we find this source of value? Many philosophers say we have to look to ourselves. Ayer, for instance, wrote that 'there are many ways in which a person's life may come to have meaning for him in itself'.[83] Anything that we find worthwhile can be a source of meaning, from child-rearing to stamp-collecting. Similarly, Nietzsche, Sartre and Camus all broadly believed that meaning and morality of life comes from within us.

There's something to this thought, but perhaps philosophers have focused too much on the individual's freedom to create meaning. In looking for meaning, we should attend to what we know about human beings in general, not just ourselves. Even if ultimately we have to choose our own meanings, we will surely have a sounder set of options if we look to what is most aligned with the better parts of human nature in general.

When people consider the possibility that the meaning of life is simply about finding what is of value in it, there is a tendency for them to respond with a disappointed, 'Is that it?' In some ways, it is indeed a sobering message, for it's quite clear that some people recognise nothing in their lives that fills it with such value, or know what would do the trick but can't attain it. In that sense, some die deeply unfulfilled, and in the absence of anything beyond this mortal life, for them there is no redemption. That is a bleak thought, one that is often ignored or downplayed by secular humanists keen to show that life without God really can be fun and happy.

Perhaps this is why many find that this kind of meaning just isn't enough. They feel what contemporary philosopher John Cottingham calls a 'need for transcendence', a connection with something beyond the 'immanent' material world that only religion can provide.[84] The problem with locating meaning in mortal life alone is not that it isn't there, but that there just isn't enough of it.

Cottingham is surely right to identify a common yearning for 'something more'. My short reply is that you can yearn as much as you like, but what you're yearning for ain't there. But the desire won't go away. I've lost count of the number of people I've heard say: 'I'm not religious, but

I am spiritual.' Few people in Britain are religious in traditional ways, with only around 10 per cent of us going to weekly church services. Nevertheless, it seems that the vast majority sense some kind of spiritual dimension to life and do not want to give it up.

The idea that spirituality is somehow necessary for a full, rounded life has quite a bit of quasi-official endorsement. In their mission statements, schools promise parents that they will look after the 'spiritual welfare' and growth of their pupils; the American military assesses 'spiritual fitness' as part of its comprehensive soldier fitness programme; while several writers have talked of the virtues of 'spiritual intelligence'.

Yet 'spiritual' remains a slippery concept. In its most basic sense, it simply contrasts with 'material'. But this distinction could be made in one of two very different ways. The first rests on a dualism between spirit and matter. The idea here is that there are more than just fundamental particles and forces of physics at work in the world. Remove all the aspects of reality described by physics and you have something left: spirit, soul or whatever. There's a lot to be said about this view, but not for it. Most philosophers and scientists would consign it to history. Even in theology, dualism is far from the universal view. It's not a trivial detail of the story that Jesus's resurrection was a bodily one: that is what provided the template for the idea of eternal life held by the early church fathers. The separate, immaterial soul was a later Greek accretion.[85]

The other way of thinking about spirituality is not in terms of stuff but value. We have our physical needs for food, shelter and health; and our material desires for wealth and possessions. But a life that revolves only around such things is an impoverished one. What we also need are morals to live by, and things that cause our spirits to soar: beauty, love, wonder and awe. None of these things seem to be captured by a scientific, materialistic way of describing the world, hence the need to think about them under a different category.

But is 'spiritual' the right one? I'm not convinced. Such are its associations that people who use it are too liable to slip into dualistic ways of thinking, seeing their spiritual life as evidence of the existence of something other than the physical world. Spirituality's association with religion also means that people are likely to see faith as the main provider of spiritual needs, and fail to see other opportunities elsewhere.

Could it be, however, that the reason why the spiritual tends to collapse into the religious is because there is something about it that just can't be captured or expressed in secular terms? The suggestion here is that this is not primarily a question of stuff or value, but the unknown, the ineffable and the mysterious. Of course, everyone accepts that there are many things that lie beyond our knowledge, or even our possible experience. That's why atheist rationalists get annoyed when they are accused of not being 'open to the unknown': they accept the limits of our knowledge as much as the religious, if not more so, since they do not seek to fill the spaces beyond science and reason with deities. But whereas the atheist materialist is simply open to the unknown, it seems to me that the spiritually inclined attempt to have a lived relationship with it. The mysteries of the universe are not just set to one side or treated as scientific puzzles to be solved. Rather, awareness of them is made a salient feature of life.

But why give what is not known such a central place in human life? It could simply be that people long to have a sense of being part of something bigger and more important than themselves. In that sense, dwelling on the infinite mysteries of the universe could be seen as an existential opiate, providing a feeling that we are important in the grand scheme of things in the face of clear evidence that we're not. A more charitable explanation is that such a spiritual life actually makes us more humble, more aware of the transitory nature of being. I suspect that both explanations can be true and it very much depends on the individual and which spiritual framework they use, with monotheistic religions tending to provide more of the false comfort.

If spirituality is indeed the attempt to have a lived relationship with the unknown, is it a good thing or a doomed, misguided enterprise? To answer this it might be helpful to look at the alternative, which found its starkest expression in the logical positivist philosophy of 1920s Vienna. According to this outlook, what cannot be verified by experience is literally meaningless. Applied to the spiritual, and colloquialised somewhat, you could say its slogan was: 'If it's ineffable, then 'effin well shut up about it.' Logical positivism may be extreme, but it represents a wider tendency to treat the unknown as a target for future human understanding which, in the meantime, is irrelevant to human experience. The spiritual tendency, in contrast, is to say that there will always be things we cannot and do not know and that a proper awareness of this is as central to the fully human life as knowledge and understanding are.

While I am sure that spiritual substances do not exist and that it's unhelpful to describe as spiritual the things that bring our ultimately physical world to profound, experiential life, I am genuinely unsure as to how much value there is in the kind of spiritual path that attempts to place the unknown at the heart of human life. What I do find interesting, however, is that understood like this, spirituality is actually antithetical to much of what passes for religion. When religion tries to explain the unknown, it arguably ceases to be spiritual at all.

Whether we embrace the unknown or not, the harsh message of existentialism remains that life can have meaning solely in the here and now, but no one can guarantee that you'll succeed in creating it, or be satisfied by it when you find it. Meaning is no exception to the rule that in an imperfect world, we have to make the best of whatever we've got.

THOUGHT AND ACTION

The Sage

—◦⦉∘⦊◦—

Minds and bodies. Thoughts and actions. Inner and outer. To think of ourselves in terms of such dualities seems like the most natural thing in the world. But what if it's not natural at all, but a mutable product of our intellectual history? The idea that these distinctions are pure cultural creations that we could do without might seem a little fanciful. More credible is the suggestion that we have come to think of them as being clearer and more absolute than they really are. For this, the blame is often laid at the door of one man: René Descartes.

One of Descartes' most eloquent accusers was Gilbert Ryle, who came up with a number of memorable phrases to describe his crimes. The most serious charge was that he established 'the myth of the ghost in the machine' as 'the official doctrine', the belief that would be the default assumption in Western thinking for centuries to come. This myth is that a person is made up of two different substances, mind and matter. But what is perhaps more damaging is what Descartes thought about the different natures of these two things. Whereas matter is public, observable and measurable, the contents of the mind are private, knowable with certainty to those who have the mind but totally inaccessible to others. And because in essence we are *res cogitans* – thinking things – rather than *res extensa* – bodily substances – we are, in effect, locked into our own private realms, interacting with the world via our bodies but located in minds housed in them.

The image this calls to mind is rather like one of the tripods in H.G. Wells's *The War of the Worlds*, which looked like 'no mere insensate machine' but a massive metallic creature with a 'strange body' and a 'brazen hood' that 'moved to and fro with the inevitable suggestion of a head looking about'. However, they were indeed mere insensate machines and the only consciousness inside them resided in their Martian operators. The 'official doctrine' suggests a similar image of our selves, living inside our bodies but not part of them. To be fair to Descartes, he recognised that this wasn't true, saying that: 'I am not merely present in my body as a sailor is present in a ship, but that I am very closely joined and, as it were, intermingled with it, so that I and the body form a unit.'[86] Nevertheless, as long as mind and body are separable, mind is what makes us who we are, and mind is private, it seems we must think of ourselves as in some sense like homunculi only temporarily residing in the body.

One effect of this way of thinking is to exaggerate the extent to which we have an 'inner' and 'outer' life. It's true that there are many things about thought and feeling that are subjective and that only we can experience for ourselves. But others can know more about our 'inner' lives than this model suggests, just as we can know less about it. Think, for example, of how common it is for someone else to notice how you are feeling before you do, and often with greater acuity. You're making tea in an agitated way, but the bad mood has just crept up on you and it takes your partner to point out that you're irritable and that the reason is that you're still simmering with resentment over the criticism of the previous cup you brewed. More serious and extreme is when someone is convinced he is deeply, truly in love when everyone else can see he's blindly besotted and there is no deep connection between him and the object of his infatuation at all. In such cases, the view from the inside is less accurate and captures less of the real person than the one from the outside.

The same general line of thought applies to the distinction between thought and action. The saying 'actions speak louder than words' doesn't tell the whole story, since it suggests that words and deeds are two ways in which our innermost thoughts, feelings and desires are expressed. But it goes deeper than this. I would argue that actions (which include what we say) don't just express thoughts, they number among them. What I mean is that if you were to give a full account of what you think, you would have to include what you do as well as what you might entertain in the privacy of your own head. So, for instance, if you make bread rather than buy it, then you must think that it's worth the effort even if you just do it and never consciously entertain the thought 'It's worth it'. Sometimes, indeed, you find out what you really think by seeing what you actually do: 'I always thought I didn't value the relationship with my parents but given that I do call them and visit them quite often, I suppose in some way I must do.'

This way of looking at things suggests what is both true and false in the idea of the unconscious that has passed into received opinion via psychoanalysis. It's true that much of what we say and do is not accompanied or directed by conscious thought, and so we can learn about the contents of our own minds by trying to observe ourselves as if from the outside. But in so doing we are not gaining access to the real, true self, which is doubly interior, being inside the inner mind. Rather, actions reveal aspects of ourselves precisely because we are not entirely defined by what goes on in the hidden recesses of our minds.

We are then 'psychosomatic wholes': not so much minds and bodies but animals that think. When we talk about thought and action, inner and outer, we are not talking about two separate domains or types of activity but two aspects of self that are deeply connected. We are then most fully ourselves when reflection and action function together. If a person without a rich inner life is like a shell without a tortoise, then the person who tries to live too much inside themselves is like a tortoise without a shell.

The Shrink

When it comes to pinning down the ingredients of well-being, I wonder whether we might have something to learn from the monks. According to *The Rule of Benedict*, one of the earliest and certainly the most influential guide to monastic life, 'Idleness is the enemy of the soul and so the brothers ought to engage in manual work at set times, and at other times in divine study'.[87] These activities were to fill the intervals between the several daily services that formed the backbone of the monk's routine. Prayer, work and study.

Time has moved on, we may or may not be believers, and anyway it transpires that over the centuries the manual work requirement slipped badly in monasteries, often surviving in purely ritualised form while most of the actual work was done by lay brothers or paid labourers. But that prescription does contain a kernel of enduring wisdom. It is simply this: it's important to pay attention to our inner life *and* be engaged with the world in a practical way.

It may sound like 'inner life' would require meditative proficiency, or following a specific spiritual path. And it may indeed include specific activities, such as reading, study or meditation. But there is an attitude of mind that is fundamental to it, and that is a kind of ongoing dialogue with ourselves. It's about reflecting, questioning, being attentive to our experience, finding our way through life by following a self-led investigative thread.

That inner dialogue makes a generous contribution to a rich and meaningful life. It's a way of cultivating some distinctive human capacities: reflection, self-awareness, problem-solving. While more external things – careers, relationships, travel – depend on the cooperation of the world and other people, this is singularly autonomous and need not be hampered by whatever else may be happening in our life. If we have a rich inner life we'll find it easier to be content with little, as our curiosity about our self and the world can be a constant source of interest.

As well as offering a peculiar delight in itself, the ability to reflect, learn and develop is essential for the self-knowledge and self-understanding that help us to steer our lives, to exercise at least a certain amount of self-governance. If we are well acquainted with our quirks and patterns we'll be better equipped to avoid their traps, and if we are clear about our values we'll be more able to live by them. Some might call this free will.

According to Aristotle, the distinctively human exercise of rationality trumped all the other potential ingredients of the good life. And for the Stoics, the sphere of human choice was the only thing in our control, therefore the only thing worth cultivating. We may not share their metaphysics, but the broader point is as relevant today as it was then.

In order to live a fully human life we need to nourish these capacities of ours. Some may question this: isn't it the case that it's these very mental capacities that hinder our ability to be in the moment in the way a cat is gloriously able to be? Perhaps we can indeed take inspiration from the cat, stretching in the sun or curling in front of the fire with no worries about the future or regrets about the past. But we can still aim to be in the moment in a distinctively human way. Being in the present in a cat-like way is more like a pathology in which memory has gone, leaving only a perpetual now.

The other side of this inner-outer coin – another way of being fully human, another source of intrinsic satisfaction – is acting on the world. Consumer society has liberated us from the need to perform endless daily chores and given us the freedom to choose what to do with our time. Literally at the flick of a switch we can get things done that in the past would have had us toiling away for hours. But according to Matthew Crawford, author of *The Case for Working with Your Hands*, the loss has been incalculable. The more we have been deprived of the opportunity to be confronted with real things in the world, the more our self-reliance has dwindled. An ethos of passive consumption has replaced one of active engagement.

Crawford suggests that the need to engage with and have some control over our environment, developing our judgement and skills in response, is an irreducible fact about humans. We are 'inherently instrumental', and 'the use of tools is really fundamental to the way human beings inhabit the world'.[88] This frustrated and long-ignored need to be 'master of one's own stuff' may have propelled the recent trends towards make-do-and-mend and grow-your-own even more than the economic downturn.

One striking example of this, Crawford reports, is that 'in the 1950s, when the focal practice of baking was displaced by the advent of cake mix, Betty Crocker learned quickly that it was good business to make the mix not quite complete. The baker felt better about her cake if she was required to add an egg to the mix.'[89] I can't help thinking of an episode of the sitcom *Father Ted*, in which housekeeper Mrs Doyle responds to a salesman's pitch about a new tea-making machine that will take the misery out of making tea by saying: 'Maybe I *like* the misery!'

Reflection and action, inner and outer, attention to self and world, are not really opposites, even though we may perceive them that way. Crawford insists that there is a significant intellectual component to practical work, since when we are trying to make or fix something we have to plan and problem-solve our way to execution. Action may inspire reflection and reflection action.

In practice, most of us will lean more one way or the other depending on temperament. Some are more doers than thinkers, some more thinkers than doers, but we'd all benefit from cultivating some balance between the two. There is no fixed formula for the right proportion: what matters is achieving a workable mix.

ON PAYING ATTENTION

The Sage

∽⟡∾

We all know about dentists with bad teeth, decorators whose homes are a mess, and, dare I add, psychotherapists who are a mass of neuroses. Even the keenest eye cannot turn its gaze on itself, and even when it tries to get around the problem with a mirror, too often the glass distorts or vision simply loses its sharpness. I'm afraid I think that philosophy is no exception to the rule. This is something of an embarrassment because philosophy prides itself on its willingness to question its basic, foundational principles and takes as one of its mottoes the inscription at the Temple of Apollo at Delphi, cited by Plato: 'Know Thyself.'

Contemporary anglophone philosophy's problem, as I see it, is that it's too wedded to the idea that its *modus operandi* is rational argument. The idea is that it proceeds by chains of reasoning, and the soundness of its conclusions are the product both of the strength of these chains and the facts from which they start. While it's undoubtedly true that this is indeed a very important part of philosophy, there is arguably something else that is at least as important, if not more so. You can call it insight or judgement, and what it relies on to work is not logical processing power, but the careful paying of attention. And this, I'd argue, is actually central to the very idea of rationality.

The claim is backed up by plenty of evidence. Look at almost all the most important 'arguments' in the history of philosophy and you find that at their core is not a deduction, but a vitally important observation.

For example, one of the most famous papers in contemporary philosophy is Thomas Nagel's 'What is it like to be a bat?' The conclusion he reaches is that it may not be possible to provide a full, objective, scientific account of what it is to be conscious. That's a big claim. But it rests mainly not on an argument, but on an observation from which the paper's title derives. We are invited to imagine what it might be like to perceive the world through echolocation, as a bat does. When we do so, we find we can't. But we are pretty sure there is something it feels like for the bat to sense the world in such a way. So we observe that there are aspects of conscious experience that cannot even be described properly by someone who does not have such experiences. What we are mainly doing here is attending to the nature of consciousness more closely, not constructing an argument.

Or take David Hume's idea that our common sense ideas about cause and effect are supported neither by logic nor experience. It should be clear that we cannot conclude from logic alone that every event must have a cause. If we believe that it nonetheless must, it can only be because that is what the evidence suggests. But attend very carefully to the simplest examples of causation. Clap your hands, and a sound is made. Did you observe the clapping cause the noise? No. All you observed was that the sound followed almost immediately after the hands came together. You know this always happens, and so you assume clapping is the cause of the sound. But this is an assumption, as it is in all cases of causation, because even under an electron microscope we never see one thing causing another, we only ever see a sequence of occurrences. This has a profound implication: our belief in cause and effect, on which not just all science but most of what we do in daily life depends, is justified neither by logic nor observation. Ironically, this conclusion is reached mainly by observation: the paying of close attention to our experience of the world.

I could give you many more examples, but hopefully the key point is clear enough already. Good philosophy depends on noticing the right things, attending to them carefully, and appreciating their significance. This matters because what is true of philosophy is true of rationality in general. To reason well about the world requires more than logical processing power. A pocket calculator can compute without understanding, but a person who does the same can never rise above the merely clever and be wise.

This is vitally important when it comes to practical reason: thinking about ethics and life choices. There are many methods that are recommended for trying to resolve difficult life choices, for example. One is to make a list of pros and cons. I'm sure this is a good idea, but it could never be possible to simply take such a list and compute the right course of action. You could try to give each factor a numerical score, but that would require more than just computation as you'd need to attend carefully to each factor and consider how important it really was. Even if you did give scores, I hope that no one would suggest that you should just tot them up and see whether the sum is positive or negative. Imagine, for example, you had twelve factors, eleven of which scored −1 and one of which scored 10. A simple sum would give you the result −1. But you can't make a general rule that you should not do something you have a very strong reason to do if there are lots of much weaker reasons why it would not be a good idea. You have to make a judgement, and to do that you don't construct an argument or do a sum, you simply have to attend to each factor in turn and see how much each really matters.

It is sometimes even the case that too much cogitation can be the problem. Often people get stuck running through the various possible options in their heads, working out different permutations, what the consequences would be and so on. At such times it can be useful to stop and ask: What really matters here? What's really at stake? Am I focusing on the right things? Too much calculation can divert us from paying attention. Philosophers, like all of us, can be like hikers so concentrated on map-reading and navigation that we don't notice the things around us that made it worth walking here in the first place.

The Shrink

'Now pay attention, please.' It sounds reproachful, as if it should be said with a stern look, or a thump on the table. But attention does matter. Left to its own devices the mind constructs a parallel world of past and future in which we can get ensnared, missing what is right in front of us – be it beautiful landscapes, warning signals, learning opportunities.

Of course there are different ways of paying attention. One of them is mindfulness, which has become very popular in recent years. Originally a kind of Buddhist meditation, its clinical applications to issues such as depression have been gathering the momentum of an avalanche.

Mindfulness meditation involves focusing on the breath while noticing other phenomena – thoughts, feelings, perceptions – arise and pass without struggling with them or getting hooked by them. Why should we want to do that? Buddhism is a spiritual path, and the primary Buddhist reason to do mindfulness meditation is to gain a direct insight into how things really are: impermanent, lacking solidity, constantly and inevitably creating suffering. That insight constitutes awakening.

The clinical rationale, on the other hand, focuses on teaching people who have suffered from depression, for instance, to catch the first occurrences of low mood and negative thoughts, before rumination establishes itself and spirals out of control. If people learn to allow even painful thoughts and feelings to come and go instead of ignoring them or trying to suppress them, their perspective can be completely altered.

As mindfulness spreads and its meaning becomes more diffuse, however, it runs the risk of acquiring the quality of a vague answer to any of life's ills. It's now invoked in so many different contexts, from mindfulness in schools to mindful leadership via all sorts of other human enter-prises, that it could look as though affixing 'mindful' to anything has become a fashionable way of giving it the appearance of extra depth. Mindfulness could come to be seen as another 'fix' that people indistinctly trust will make them healthier and happier, or magically solve career dilemmas, or even improve their sex life (as I recently read in a magazine).

But mindfulness is also simply a way of attending to experience with attention and acceptance, and there are at least two sound reasons to practise it even if you're not after enlightenment or suffering from a particular clinical problem. The first is aesthetic: it just is pleasing to see more facets of what is around us more vividly. Most of the time, caught as we are in our ruminations, we completely miss things like the patterns of light on the wall, or the redness of autumn berries on the trees. Noticing these textures makes for a richer and fuller life experience.

The Vietnamese Zen teacher Thich Nhat Hanh writes poetically about how a mindful awareness transforms the experience of daily life by helping us to notice the wonder of everything around us, not just the beauty of nature. He teaches that we should bring that mindful attention to everything we do, starting with the simplest things – washing the dishes, making a cup of tea: 'Wash the dishes relaxingly, as though each bowl is an object of contemplation. Consider each bowl as sacred. Follow your breath to prevent your mind from straying. Do not try to hurry to get the job over with. Consider washing the dishes the most important thing in life. Washing the dishes is meditation. If you cannot wash the dishes in mindfulness, neither can you meditate while sitting in silence.'[90]

The other reason is pragmatic. As Buddhist atheist Stephen Batchelor writes, we normally drift along 'unaware on a surge of habitual impulses'.[91] We are so glued to our thoughts and feelings that we don't realise they're just transient mental states. So we mindlessly allow them to lead us around, dictating what we do even if it's often far from a wise course of action.

Becoming mindful in this sense means becoming more aware of the kaleidoscope of thoughts and feelings within ourselves, of the first flickers of hurt, anger, self-pity. If we learn to catch these stirrings as they arise we should be better placed to exert some control over how we respond to things. We should be more able to choose the values we wish to act on. Of course we might come to endorse our initial judgement that something was good or bad, but at least we would have escaped the automaticity of our reaction, and that can only be a good thing.

Do we really need meditation to develop some mindfulness skills? The short answer is no, although practising sitting quietly focusing on your breathing can help. (The long answer would depend on what you're trying to achieve.) In Acceptance and Commitment Therapy, there are several exercises to help people to make room for what they're actually experiencing while taking a step back from their thoughts. Of course none of this talk of acceptance and stepping back means you shouldn't try to change situations that need to be changed or attempt to correct your shortcomings, just that this is better done in a spirit of acceptance of what is.

It's interesting to compare this with another way of paying attention, which has become known as *flow*. Mihalyi Csikszentmihalyi writes that this occurs when we have clear goals, immediate feedback, and our skills and challenges are appropriately matched, when we find our task intrinsically rewarding and give it our full attention. Then we tend to get lost in the experience, forget our self, lose track of time.

In some ways this state seems the opposite of mindfulness: instead of being aware of every ripple in our subjective experience, we become altogether unaware of it, absorbed as we are in what we are doing. But like mindfulness, flow is about controlling attention, creating order in our ordinarily chaotic consciousness. Instead of wasting energy worrying about our daily niggles and frustrations, which is what our minds tend to do left to their own devices, consciousness is ordered by concentrating on a task.[92] And it's not just about peak experiences. Csikszentmihalyi states clearly that everyone can have more flow in their life by creating the conditions outlined above.

The thread that joins mindfulness and flow is the value of being able to direct our attention and act consciously instead of being unreflectively pushed around by the constant stream of impulses running through our minds. That ability is not a panacea: neither mindfulness nor flow alone will tell us how to live or help us to make decisions or solve our problems. But it's most definitely something worth developing, which could make a real difference as we negotiate life's twists and turns.

Mindful attention is not something to resort to only when life is problematic, when we need to be lifted from the sometimes grinding quotidian concerns. An attitude of openness and curiosity to our own inner experience and to things big and small in the world around us is enriching, and best adopted as a way of life. Combined with compassion, as the Buddhists advised, it can take us a long way towards goodness and wisdom.

Part Two

Part Two

PSYCHOLOGY FOR PHILOSOPHERS

Julian Baggini

For the first few millennia of human civilisation, there was no distinction between philosophy and psychology. The study of the human mind had many branches – practical, theoretical, empirical, logical – but all were attached to the same root. It was only in the nineteenth century that, like a bramble, a branch then known as experimental psychology started setting down its own roots. Over time, the differences between this scientific study of how the mind actually works and what went on in the rest of philosophy became too great to ignore. There was of course no precise moment when the two subjects went their separate ways but there was a kind of filing for divorce in 1913, when 107 German, Austrian and Swiss philosophers signed a petition demanding that no more philosophy professorships should be given to experimental psychologists. Much as they welcomed 'the gratifying advance of this discipline', it was an 'independent field which demands the full energy of a scholar'. The 'experimental investigation of mental life' needed its own departments and professors, leaving philosophy to the philosophers.[93]

The divorce was amicable and in many ways was in the best interests of both parties. But it came at a cost. As a couple, philosophy and psychology are guardians to nothing less than the good life. If we want to know how to live, we need the insights of philosophers and psychologists, which is difficult when they are no longer living together and don't even talk as much as they should.

What made the marriage so valuable was that it enabled a harmonious cohabitation of issues of fact and value. Take human reason as an example. Philosophy articulates the principles of logic, sound argument and robust inference, which are truths about rationality, but not facts about how people actually think. Philosophy then endorses the value of these principles, insisting that this is how we should strive to reason, in many areas, if not all. Psychology, in contrast, has told us an enormous amount about how the mind actually works, and in so doing has showed that the human brain very rarely comes to its conclusions by following logical methods. The brain uses all sorts of quick and dirty shortcuts, 'heuristics', which do the job of coming swiftly to the right conclusion and often enough to enable us to survive, but which lack the reliability of sound logical arguments. If you consider the issue of human reason to be concerned with how we can best utilise our rational capacities, it would seem that you need an ideal of how we should strive to reason; insights into the biases, tricks and shortcuts the mind actually uses; as well as the rules that govern whether an inference is actually valid or not. Now, alas, if you want all that you have to study two subjects.

This division between *fact* and *value*, between *is* and *ought*, is even more problematic when it comes to living the good life. We surely do need psychology to provide a factual, evidential basis to ideas we might have about what kinds of life are better or worse for human beings. A great deal of philosophy rests on assumptions about human nature. Before psychology existed as a distinctive discipline, this may have been unavoidable. But now there is no excuse for making sweeping claims about human nature that are not backed up by facts established by psychologists. As a more or less random example, take this claim by Karl Marx: '[T]he more the worker exhausts himself, the more powerful the alien world of objects he creates over and against himself becomes, the poorer he and his inner world become, the less there is that belongs to him as his own.'[94] This is part of what Marx meant by 'alienation', a key concept in his political philosophy. It should be clear that this is an empirical claim about the effect of work on the human psyche. If anyone is going to maintain this claim today, it would be absurd for them to do so without taking into account the evidence from psychology as to whether or not it stands up. In short, to the extent that philosophical claims about the right way to live rest on beliefs about human nature, philosophy needs psychology if it is not to be empty speculation. Your claims about how things ought to be cannot be taken seriously if you don't understand how they actually are.

On the one hand, you cannot draw any direct conclusions about the way things ought to be solely on the basis of an understanding of how they are. This is the bind psychology finds itself in, having hived off the fact part of the study of the human mind but left behind the values. This is becoming increasingly apparent in the growth of positive psychology, which is the laudable attempt to balance psychology's traditional focus on what makes minds go wrong with attention to what makes them go right. However, when it tries to do this it finds itself taking for granted that we know what it means for things to go right. Most obviously, positive psychologists have done a lot of research into what makes people happy, but they are simply unable to say whether or not being happy is an appropriate goal in life. It might seem obvious that it is, but one example alone should be sufficient to show why it is not: religion. A lot of research suggests that being religious tends to make people happy. This is disputed, and at the very least it does seem true that some forms of religion might make you unhappy. But what should be clear is that, whatever turns out to be the case, knowing how happy a religion makes people does not give you a reason to be religious or not. If you were a devout Catholic, you would see no reason why you should change your mind if you found out Catholics were less happy than atheists. From your point of view, all that would show is that non-believers were smiling fools, which is exactly how happy-clappy Christians appear to more sober atheists. In short, to the extent that psychological claims about the right way to live rest on beliefs about what is good, psychology needs philosophy if it is not to confuse description with prescription, facts with values. Your claims about how things ought to be cannot be taken seriously if you understand *only* how they actually are.

This is/ought distinction is even more important, but also more complicated, when it comes to psychology's therapeutic offspring. Psychotherapy operates in a strange hinterland between facts and values. In a sense, its very existence assumes a set of values: the desirability of helping people to live their lives to the full. Yet at the same time many, if not most, psychotherapists do not feel that it's their job to seriously question or interrogate their clients' ideas about what a full life is. Like parents with their children, therapists don't mind what their clients do, as long as it makes them happy. But also like parents, this isn't quite true, but it's only when the path chosen is clearly deviant that they'll pipe up and say so.

In practice, this means that between psychotherapy and philosophy there is one tension and one conflict of goals. The tension is that philosophy wants to interrogate values as much as possible, therapy wants to leave them alone as much as possible. The conflict is that therapy aims at the restoration of a person to full functioning, whereas philosophy aims to find the truth. This conflict is what has made me very suspicious of philosophical counselling (see the chapter 'Philosophy for psychotherapy'). I remember, for instance, being very perturbed to hear one philosophical counsellor suggest that their job was to find out what a client thought and then match that with the philosophers who might be able to articulate that world view more fully. The idea that you should cherry-pick philosophers to bolster what you already think seems to me to be contrary to the philosophical spirit. But what you could do (and to be fair, this might be what the counsellor in question really meant) is to take the point of connection between what the client already thinks and the philosophical canon as the start of an investigation. But you would not be doing philosophy if you appropriated philosophical ideas and texts purely in the service of feeling better. Philosophical lines of thought should be followed wherever they lead, no matter how they make you feel. They should not be plotted backwards, from an endpoint that you want to reach. Philosophy is exploration, not a guided tour. Philosophical counselling, when done well, is this kind of exploration, one that continually relates philosophy to problems of living but does not simply try to appropriate its resources to solve them at any price.

If you are serious about thinking about how we should live, it therefore seems clear that philosophy, psychology and psychotherapy all have things to offer and that they will be most useful when in combination. We need to consider what we want and what is possible; facts about how we are and values about how we want to be; what is true and what enables us to live more fully; intellectual under-standing and practical wisdom. It's a kind of accident of intellectual history that these questions have become sepa-rated and have become the specialised concerns of three different disciplines. But we can put them back together, and that is part of what this book is about.

Research suggests

The philosophical sensibility is perhaps most obviously useful when it comes to making sense of the constant stream of research findings that inform our ideas about how we should live. Some of the reasons for caution are obvious and well-advertised, especially by psychologists themselves. The main one is that you should never jump to conclusions on the basis of just one study. Nonetheless, there are several findings that appear to have been substantiated by numerous, independent studies. In headline terms, a typical summary of what psychologists have found over recent decades would include the fact that the major determinants of human well-being are health and the quality of relationships; that wealth provides diminishing returns for happiness, helping a lot as people rise out of poverty but contributing little or nothing once they are moderately affluent; that optimism is better for you than pessimism; that having a religious faith or sense of higher purpose makes you happier; and that inequality of wealth or status adversely affects both mental and physi-cal health.

All of these things, if true, would be important data for anyone interested in trying to explore what is a good life for human beings. But as Ben Goldacre, a tireless exposer of sloppy research and even sloppier interpretation of it, puts it in his popular T-shirt slogan, 'I think you'll find it's a bit more complicated than that'. So often we are presented with reports on research as though it was clear-cut when it rarely is. The correct verb for research is almost always 'suggests' rather than 'shows', and suggestions can be good or bad.

We need to start with the experiments themselves. The most obvious point is that experiments are by their nature usually highly artificial constructs. They need to be, because their goal is to isolate variables, such as the difference it makes whether one, two or twenty people are around you when someone appears to need your help. You can't control these variables in the real world, so you need to construct an artificial scenario. The problem is that in doing so you may isolate some variables but introduce another that you can't control for: the difference it might make that the situation is in some sense artificial, taking place in a university psychology lab, for instance. So it's always questionable how much laboratory-based research findings tell us about how people act in ordinary life. You need to look carefully at how each individual experiment was designed to even make a reasonable judgement about how critical this might be.

Experimental results may also be skewed by the nature

of the experimental subjects. It's a sad truth that for obvious practical reasons, much research that purports to tell us about human nature in general is actually conducted almost exclusively on young, white, middle-class American undergraduates. Having been a British version of one of these, and living next door to nine of them, I can say with some confidence that these people are not normal. So we again always have to ask: Who were these experiments conducted on, and are they representative of the rest of us in the relevant respects?

Let's just assume that doubts about experimental design have been satisfied. The next problem is working out just what a finding means. Scientists have a mantra, a kind of eternal truth: correlation is not causation. If you found that more Scottish football fans suffer from seasonal affective disorder (SAD) than Spanish ones, then you would probably see straight away that being a fan of a Scottish football team is not likely to be the causal factor, but living at a higher latitude with darker winters. Supporting Rangers or Celtic may be *correlated* with SAD but it's very unlikely to be its *cause*, unless the team goes through a particularly bad winter slump in form.

In other cases, however, the correlation/causation distinction is less obvious. Churchgoing may well be correlated with happiness, for example (although the evidence isn't clear), but that by itself would not show that being religious causes people to be happier. It might be that merely going to church does the trick, whether you're religious or not, and that non-churchgoing believers are no happier than anyone else. It might also be that churchgoing isn't the critical factor at all, and that simply being the member of any active community group would do the trick. Recent research has also suggested that being religious has more of a positive effect on those who live in more religious societies, suggesting that it's fitting in and feeling connected that counts, rather than belief.[95]

Once you become aware of this, however, you quickly see that almost all studies that suggest links between events, situations, beliefs or dispositions and measures of welfare do not establish the causal nature of that link. For instance, BBC Radio has just conducted a very large study that linked tendency to depression with rumination and self-blame.[96] Researchers came up against the common problem of the arrow of causation: even if there is a causal link, is it that feeling depressed causes people to self-blame and ruminate, or is it that rumination and self-blame cause depression? They concluded that depression was the effect not the cause, but even with the huge amount of data collected, they can't be sure whether rumination itself is the problem or only certain kinds of rumination. Also, because rumination and self-blame went together so often, it wasn't certain which of the pair was most responsible for depression.

These complications help explain why even the most robust, well-established statistical links need to be treated with caution. One example is the link between optimism and all sorts of positive outcomes: more health, more happiness, longer life. The research here does seem to be robust. But does this show optimism is good for you? Not necessarily, and here's why. Imagine I divide a group of children into boys and girls and I then see how able they are to reach a high handle. I would find the boys tend to do better than the girls. Does this show that being a boy is the cause of being able to reach high handles? Of course not. Being tall is what matters, and it just so happens that being a boy means you are more likely to be taller. The problem is that the data has not been properly disaggregated: broken up into its most basic parts. Male and female are treated as the fundamental categories whereas, in fact, they are not.

Something similar might be going on with the optimism research. What causes all these better outcomes might be people's willingness and ability to look for solutions and do what they can to make the future better. It seems very likely that if you divide people up into optimists and pessimists, then you will find more of these kind of people in the optimism group than the pessimism one. But this is not because being optimistic is the critical factor, simply that it tends to be associated with the critical factor, just as being male is more associated with being tall than being female. This could be vitally important, because optimism may sometimes work against this key factor. There is a certain kind of blind optimism that assumes the future will be good, which makes people less, not more likely to look for solutions and do what they can to make the future better.

Insufficient disaggregation is not the only reason why causation is incorrectly inferred from correlation. Another is that causes are often assumed to be fixed when they are not. Go back to the gender example, for instance. Imagine that it's shown to be true that fathers are less inclined to spend time at home with their children than women. The problem is that we would still not know whether this is an inevitable feature of human nature or the result of social norms and conventions. Indeed, it might be impossible to know what contribution nature and nurture make because as soon as a child comes out of the womb, it is exposed to all sorts of influences that reflect deeply-rooted social conventions. So we might know that men are less child-centred than women, but we would not know whether this is inevitable. We always need to ask the question: If one thing leads to another, is that because of an intrinsic link between the two or simply because current circumstances facilitate that link? This issue is particularly pressing when it comes to causes of depression, for example. It seems very likely indeed that many things tend to cause depression only because the social context makes those things problematic. For instance, several studies have suggested a link between homosexuality and suicide. But it seems much more likely that what drives some homosexuals to take their own lives is the intolerance and persecution they face, not homosexuality itself.

When it comes to interpreting what research means for you as an individual, you also have to be very careful to remember that research of this kind only ever tells you what tends to be the case, on average. Rumination may not make *you* depressed, even if it does so for most people. Take any individual homosexual and they are not likely to be depressed. You might be more content if you were a little more pessimistic, lowering expectations, even if in general most people are not optimistic enough. Too often research is summarised as though it applied to everyone, or everyone in a group. Perhaps most pernicious of all are the gender-based findings. We can say with some confidence, for instance, that no research has ever found that men are greater risk-takers, more promiscuous, less socially competent than women. All that has been claimed is that more men than women take risks, are promiscuous and lack social skills. That tells you nothing about any individual man or woman. At most it tells you that if you know nothing about a person other than their gender, certain things are more likely than others. To think it told you anything more would be like confusing climate data with a weather forecast, making the mistake of thinking that because it rains more in March than in August, you can leave your umbrella at home during an English summer.

All of the issues I've mentioned so far follow straightforwardly from a proper understanding of the use of statistics and the limitations of experimental techniques. However, there is another cluster of problems with the interpretation of research that is not as appreciated as it should be. This concerns the difference between what we know and what we do about it. Consider, for instance, the difference between explanation and justification. If we go back to the gender example, what would it mean if it were the case that men are less interested in active parenting than women? Not, I would hope, that fathers around the world use this research to justify not doing their bit. 'Sorry, darling, I don't want to change the baby's nappy. It's a guy thing.' Gender differences might explain why some people are more inclined to do some things than others, but it does not follow that they are justified in not doing so. If you are more inclined than your flatmate to let the house get dirty, that does not justify you leaving all the cleaning to him. Even if we cannot help having certain inclinations, we can decide what we do about them, and there is simply no reason to assume that merely having a preference or tendency justifies always pandering to it.

There are also related issues around what we should do in the light of discoveries about cognitive biases: distortions of thinking that occur naturally, beyond our conscious control. Take confirmation bias, which is the tendency to notice evidence that supports what you believe and not notice or ignore evidence that goes against it. This is far from a purely intellectual problem. If you become convinced, wrongly, that your partner is having an affair, for example, confirmation bias will make you notice all the things that fit in with that theory and will even distort neutral or counter-evidence. So, that loving bunch of flowers becomes a sign of guilt. Similarly, depression can feed off a tendency to see everything that happens as confirmation that people don't like you, that you're seriously ill, that you're a failure or whatever it is that brings you down.

The problem is that when psychologists identify such biases, they often point out that we can't help but have them. Sometimes that just isn't true: with practice, we can overcome some of them. But even when we cannot, that does not mean that we can't take steps to mitigate or counteract their most pernicious effects. Simply knowing about confirmation bias can prod you to make an effort to look for evidence that goes against what you believe. Knowing that people tend to overestimate the abilities of physically attractive people can make you more careful when interviewing a job candidate not to be swayed by mere appearances.

There is one more issue around the difference between what we know and what we do that has more of a social dimension, and that concerns relative importance. I became alerted to that when I conducted a small survey on complaining. I found that there was a significant difference between the patterns of complaint of men and women. But there was an even greater difference between Americans and Britons. This meant that an American woman complained more like an American man than she did a British woman. The realisation that came over me when I saw this was that even if there are real and abiding differences between the sexes, they may be less important than cultural differences. So simply knowing that there are such gender differences does not tell you anything about how much point there is in trying to counter them.

Marx famously observed that philosophers had only interpreted the world when the point was to change it. The problem with psychology, it seems, is that it's trying too hard to change it when its main task is simply to understand it. But although drawing conclusions about how we should live from research in psychology is a tricky business, it would be foolish to ignore the insights that have emerged from the scientific, experimental investigation of the mind. The trick is to use the research but not to make too much of it. That has been our goal in this book. We have tried to keep up with the best evidence from psychology, always mindful of the need to be cautious, to interpret, and to be careful about drawing practical implications from factual claims. You could sum up the thinking behind this as the principle that it just isn't possible to base a model of the right way to live on research findings alone, but that any model of the right way to live needs to be at least consistent with what we know about actual human thinking and behaviour. The good life needs to be compatible with what psychology tells us, but psychology cannot tell us what the good life is.

PHILOSOPHY FOR PSYCHOTHERAPY

Antonia Macaro

❧

Problems in living

Life's full of suffering, whether avoidable and self-inflicted or a completely inevitable consequence of being human. From practical issues like career choices or interpersonal conflict to big fuzzy ones like meaning and purpose via all manner of ethical dilemmas that have no clear answer, problems get in our way all the time no matter how much we strive to dodge them.

That's not to say life is *only* suffering: of course it can also be joy, excitement, sharing, learning and other wonderful exhilarating things. But the fact remains that some suffering is inevitable. If we're lucky enough we may avoid some adversities such as divorce, loneliness, poverty and war. But even the most blessed lives cannot escape old age, illness and death. The first noble truth of Buddhism – that life is suffering – cannot be faulted.

One response is to seek spiritual guidance, in the hope of being infused with a new vision of things that will make our burden feel lighter. Religions manage to put a spin on suffering by placing it into a larger perspective that somehow fills it with meaning: karma and rebirth, heaven and hell. But to get the relief you have to buy into the dogma, and many feel the price is too high.

Alternatively, you could try to cultivate non-attachment. Instead of trying to achieve happiness by satisfying as many desires as possible, you adopt the opposite policy of minimising the desires. If you don't value the things of the world much, you'll suffer less when you are deprived of them. Buddhism and Stoicism, for instance, recommend this approach. But it's hard to pull off, and if we become too detached from other people and the world around us we may pay the price of losing depth of experience, particularly in personal relationships.

In our happiness-focused times, however, we are more likely to see suffering as a problem awaiting a technological fix, something that could potentially be eliminated through some kind of therapy. It's only a matter of finding the right one, which will help us to unburden ourselves and bask in perpetual happiness – or at least have an easy ride through life. Will it be years of psychoanalysis to unlock the secrets of our childhood or twelve sessions of CBT to rid us of our dysfunctional beliefs? Or a course of medication?

Somewhere, somehow, problems in living became pathologies to be treated. According to Thomas Szasz, author of *The Myth of Mental Illness*, it all began with Freud, who 'conquered what is in effect the human condition by annexing it in its entirety to the medical profession'.[97] But much as he wanted his method to be scientific,

Freud was also aware that 'In psychoanalysis, alas, every-thing is different [from medicine]. Nothing takes place in a psychoanalytic treatment but an interchange of words between the patient and the analyst.'[98]

Lacanian therapist Darian Leader has talked of 'the gulf that separates those traditions of therapy that are based on humanistic or spiritual values and those based on a belief in medical-style intervention',[99] clearly counting psychoa-nalysis among the former. The sentiment is sound, but it sits uneasily with the language of 'patients' and 'treatment' that is a staple of many forms of psychotherapy including psychoanalysis. Therapists are inviting misunderstanding if they continue to help themselves to this kind of medical terminology.

Whether it was because of Freud or despite him, how-ever, medical conditions have been swallowing up more and more of what used to be just life problems, like an uncon-tainable oil spill. The process continues apace through suc-cessive editions of the American Psychiatric Association's *Diagnostic and Statistical Manual of Mental Disorders* (also known as DSM, currently in its fourth incarnation).

The much-awaited DSM-5 is currently in prepara-tion. From what has transpired so far, it seems we can look forward to further medicalisation of normality. To take only one example, under the proposed new criteria some-one may be diagnosed with major depression following a bereavement if their grief 'symptoms' last beyond as little as two weeks. This would inevitably colour our perception of grief, turning into a pathology what is a normal process, moulded by culture and individuality, that people go through while they come to terms with their loss.

We are strangely reassured by diagnoses, sensitive to the peculiar soothing of being able to name the problem we've been struggling with and knowing we're in the company of others. Learning you're suffering from social anxiety disorder when you thought you were just shy can be comforting by legitimising your experience while shifting the blame to your brain chemistry – nothing to do with *you*.

But the comfort of medicalisation also has a price tag. Apart from potential dependence on medication that may do little good and yet have harmful side-effects, it can create the illusion of a simple cure, encouraging passivity and denial of responsibility. If you expect a doctor or therapist to fix your problems, be it with a pill or a magic wand, you will be less motivated to make an effort, to do your bit to make progress.

No therapy will free us of life's pains. But if problems in living can't be eliminated, it may at least be possible to contain the self-inflicted kind of suffering and learn to deal better with the inevitable kind. This is essentially a search for wisdom, one that we would all be well advised to undertake. But what resources can we draw on? Should we read the works of the great philosophers, go into therapy or both? When you need help or guidance through life's choppy stretches, should you resort to the shrink or the sage?

What can psychotherapy do for you?

Psychotherapy is not a profession. By that I mean that whether or not it is a *profession*, it's certainly not *a* profession. The singular noun is misleading. It's more like a raucous rabble of disparate approaches, based on completely different assumptions and methods, which just won't sit together quietly for long. There are many kinds, some themselves umbrellas for diverse practices, and I could not even begin to list them here.

Then there is counselling, which originally was a distinctive approach based on the work of Carl Rogers but increasingly comes in the same flavours as psychotherapy. Although some distinctions can be made between the two, I believe the overlap is greater and so I use the terms interchangeably.

The image of psychotherapy that has seeped into the public perception comes from psychoanalysis. You can picture it: the silent analyst, the patient on the couch, revisiting childhood, interpreting dreams, unearthing the unconscious. But all that is only part of what goes on in psychotherapy. There is a hugely varied range of approaches, from transpersonal therapies that border on the religious ('soul-making at work', as the Institute of Psychosynthesis puts it) to body psychotherapies, which aim at 'releasing' the early traumas they believe are 'trapped' in the body.

The other central character in the therapy double act is Cognitive-Behaviour Therapy (CBT). The main idea is the tight connection between how we think, what we do, and how we feel. By identifying and changing unhelpful thoughts and behaviours, moods and feelings can also change. CBT is short-term and active. It uses many different techniques including mood and thought diaries, behavioural experiments, and lots of homework.

While CBT is celebrated and at the moment generously funded, it's also widely accused of being 'only a sticking plaster'. Now there is something to the point that it's often useful to examine the whole network of thoughts and emotions from which certain problems have arisen. On the other hand there is also value in targeting particular complaints. Often pragmatic action in the world is required, and a local, limited intervention may, for whatever reason, be the only one possible.

But nowadays there are fewer and fewer purists, and a pick-and-mix attitude prevails. Many therapists and counsellors describe themselves as 'integrative' and help themselves to ingredients from various pots to make up their own particular recipes: take a bunch of psychodynamics, add a pinch of Gestalt with a generous sprinkling of CBT together with Rogers's core conditions, *et voilà*. And why not? Different therapies have different strengths, so why shouldn't we take what works from each of them? It's a little more complicated than that, however, as not all approaches have the same understanding of what 'working' means, so it's not clear that this really makes sense without some kind of coherent framework.

Despite the integrative drift, it seems to me there is a

battle going on for the very soul of therapy. The main issue is whether psychotherapy and counselling should aim to be evidence-based methods, directed at producing measurable changes in symptoms, attitudes and behaviours, as is increasingly expected, or instead a kind of conversation about how to deal with life's challenges. CBT is currently winning on the evidence-based front, and other therapies are bound to be pushed into adapting to some extent.

Some do swim against the tide. Existential therapists tend to eschew diagnoses and techniques, focusing instead on each individual's unique experience of being human – values, assumptions, worldviews. Emmy van Deurzen has long championed psychotherapy as an exploration of how to live. For Irvin Yalom, the issues that people struggle with and bring to therapy are in one way or another rooted in the givens of existence – death, freedom and responsibility, aloneness, the search for meaning.

Ernesto Spinelli explicitly questions the mainstream assumption 'that therapy is both a special and necessary "cure" for human misery and that therapists ... are the qualified agents of that "cure"'.[100] Spinelli rejects the view that the aim of psychotherapy is to bring about measurable shifts in attitudes or behaviour, and instead sees its task as that of elucidating the client's way of being, the experience of 'what and how it is for me to exist'.[101] This enterprise may well lead to changes, but these are not directed by the therapist.

At the moment psychotherapy dons both hats, its identity shifting awkwardly between science and art – a technology to help with difficulties like anxiety or depression, which interfere with functioning in the world, and a dialogue about life and ethics. There is a widespread assumption that therapy should belong to one camp or the other. But there appears to be room and a need for both kinds of activities – whether or not it's therapy as we know it that would best fulfil it.

Of course the two strands are not mutually exclusive. They'd better not be, as there is a vast grey area between them. Some of those who are struggling with debilitating complaints may also benefit from a deeper exploration of meaning and value in their life, while many of those who wish to deal with things more wisely could often do with practical tools to put the desired changes into practice.

A therapeutic perspective that usefully combines a focus on values to live by with exercises to facilitate their expression is Acceptance and Commitment Therapy (ACT). It's part of the so-called third wave CBT but in many ways in a category of its own. In ACT, negative mental states are normal for a human mind. Steve Hayes, originator of the approach, calls this the *assumption of destructive normality*.[102] Getting rid of negative feelings is a fundamentally misguided aim. It can't be done. So our aims should not be framed in terms of mental states. Instead, we should learn to relate to our constantly shifting experience with mindfulness. By doing this we gain enough distance from the sometimes turbulent influence of our emotions to get on with what we truly value in life – whatever we may be feeling at any given time.

This emphasis on values and action rather than feelings is shared by an older, less well known approach, developed by Japanese psychiatrist Shoma Morita. The central principle of Morita Therapy is that we cannot directly control our internal experience, so we should accept its fluctuations and take constructive action. Feelings fade in time anyway, and it would be more harmful to spend too much energy trying to control them.

Depending on which approach you choose, psychotherapy may be one place where you can examine the values, dilemmas, and existential issues that arise from your daily life. But whether you get good guidance on these matters depends very much on the individual therapist. If this is the kind of exploration you want, therapy can only take you so far (and it may end up taking you in a completely different direction). So why not turn to the specialists in wisdom? Would you be better off with philosophy?

What can philosophy do for you?

In a competition for the most popular philosophy with therapeutic applications, the Stoics would almost certainly win. One reason for their popularity is that despite their rather high-minded doctrines they addressed questions of daily life in engaging and quotable ways. As philosopher Richard Sorabji put it to me, it's an ethical philosophy that 'taps you on the shoulder'.

Another reason is that Aaron Beck and Albert Ellis, founders respectively of CBT and its cousin REBT (Rational-Emotive Behaviour Therapy) were influenced by Stoic ideas. Epictetus' view that 'it is not the things themselves that disturb people but their judgements about those things'[103] is often credited with being the foundation on which those therapies were built.

The Stoics did indeed say many things that could help us to live more wisely. Seneca's letters, for instance, address questions that sooner or later are bound to concern most of us. But Stoicism is also a complex and demanding philosophy, revolving around the idea that our reason is a fragment of a divine rational mind that organises the whole of nature. Rational choice is the only thing that is in our power and that we should value unconditionally. The emotions stirred in us by the desire of worldly things, on the other hand, are nothing but disturbances created by false attributions of value, and should be avoided. Taking non-attachment to a new level, Epictetus wrote: 'If you kiss your child, or your wife, say to yourself that it is a human being that you are kissing; and then you will not be disturbed if either of them dies.'[104]

Should we subscribe to such a stark doctrine? Inner tranquillity is a good thing, but adopting a blanket policy of detachment to get it might lead to avoidance of emotional closeness for fear of future suffering, and an impoverished life narrowly focused on avoiding pain. Anyway, it's now clear that far from hindering rational decision-making, emotions are an integral part of it (although of course they can also get us into trouble, and should be checked).

There is certainly much we can learn from the Stoics, but it may be wise to do some cherry-picking. This approach is endorsed by Richard Sorabji and ultimately by at least some of the Stoics themselves. Some Stoic perspectives that may be helpful to most of us include regularly asking ourselves 'Does it really matter?', reminding ourselves that a lot of the things we commonly worry about are not that important, and that we don't have to follow our evolved desires slavishly; the habit of monitoring our emotions, remembering that we have at least some influence on how we think and consequently on how we feel; and accepting that much of what happens to us in life is beyond our control.

The Stoics have also bequeathed us some useful practices, which Pierre Hadot likens to spiritual exercises.[105] One of these is self-examination: in the morning we give thought to the values we want to live by; in the evening we ask ourselves where we went wrong and what progress we made.

Then there was the *praemeditatio malorum* (meditation on future evils), which involved anticipating disasters – suffering, poverty, death – to keep the fragility of life at the front of our minds and remind ourselves that what could be taken away from us (which is everything apart from reason) should mean nothing to us. This practice, refreshingly unorthodox in a climate where optimism is *de rigueur*, could also help us to keep a sense of perspective and appreciate what we have. But we should beware: unless we do this in the right frame of mind we could end up anxious and depressed rather than serene.

Ancient philosophy is such a gold mine for wise advice because of its focus on living a good life. We have already sung the praises of Aristotle. In later philosophies the nuggets that are clearly relevant to living wisely are fewer and further between and have to be extracted more laboriously. Leaving aside the universally loved exception of Montaigne, there are long arguments to be had about which philosophers fare better – whether Wittgenstein or Heidegger, for instance, has more to say on how to live.

I'll put my cards on the table here and declare that Wittgenstein has my vote. In particular, I found his distinction between reasons and causes relevant to the practice of psychotherapy. If I asked you why you like listening to a particular piece of music, say, you might reply that it makes you feel peaceful, or that you admire the intricate interweaving of the parts. Those would be your reasons. What you probably wouldn't do is launch into an exposition of the patterns of sound waves and neural activity that caused your experience of liking. Reasons are part of a chain of beliefs and desires through which we explain our actions. Causal claims, on the other hand, are unconnected to the agent's experience and are best seen as hypotheses requiring empirical investigation.

Reasons and causes are easily mixed up. While finding some of Freud's ideas interesting, Wittgenstein thought he had got himself – and psychoanalysis – into a muddle by confusing the two. Freud sought to explain symptoms and behaviours through unconscious causal mechanisms. A young lady's hysteria is interpreted as being caused by repressed sexual feelings, say. But this is neither a reason (it's external to her experience) nor a cause (it's not an empirical hypothesis). We are left with speculation. This confusion continues to be perpetuated by many therapists. That is why people often mistakenly think all psychotherapy is about uncovering hidden causes when more often it's about working with reasons.

Working with people with alcohol problems, you soon find out that the most pressing question for many of them is 'I want to know why I drink'. But the why is ambiguous, as it could invite an answer in terms of reasons or causes. What people wish to know is what remote factors (genes, upbringing and so on) caused them to drink. That is an interesting question, but in the context of counselling and psychotherapy it's not normally the most useful. Even if we could somehow obtain that information, how would it help? On the other hand, once we have uncovered people's reasons for drinking – be it boredom, stress, or whatever – we can work on elaborating them, identifying their implications, challenging them.

Matters are much more complicated than can be captured in a brief summary. There are certainly times when causal explanations are relevant in psychotherapy. If someone's actions were caused by an organic illness, for instance (as in the case of the paedophile I mention in 'Are you responsible?'), then any dialogue about reasons would clearly be superseded by the relevant treatment. There is also the problem that we can be pitifully and extensively self-deceived about our own reasons why we act as we do, as more and more studies are now showing. But whatever the exact relationship between reasons and causes turns out to be, it's useful to be aware of the distinction. It may not always be clear-cut, but at least in therapy it's usually much more fruitful to focus on reasons than causes.

Even seemingly obscure philosophical distinctions can help to shed light on life issues. If you want guidance in reflecting philosophically on problems and dilemmas, the relatively recent practice of philosophical counselling may be able to help. Just like psychotherapy, it's misleading to refer to philosophical counselling in the singular. Some incarnations claim kinship with therapy, others stand proudly on their own, but all aim at putting philosophy into action. This is very different from giving a lecture, holding a tutorial, or delivering some kind of secular sermon (although some philosophical counsellors do rely on using relevant philosophical theories as props). It should facilitate reflection, elicit and develop concerns, explore values and conceptual networks, help people to clarify the reasons for and consequences of their actions.

A useful label for this process, which I take from Ran Lahav's early writings, is *worldview interpretation*.[106] The idea is that everything we do – our choices, hopes, plans, reactions, feelings – expresses a kind of philosophy about ourselves and the world. This is by no means a fully worked out, consistent philosophy of life; it's more like an implicit, perhaps contradictory, set of views about what matters, what to aim for, what to expect of others. We can shed light on our everyday problems by probing it, exploring its implications and ramifications, bringing assumptions closer to the surface.

Some psychotherapies of a more philosophical bent, which regard themselves as standing in the realm of ethics rather than science, might be able to do something similar. But philosophical counselling is right to proclaim its difference from therapy as we know it in being an unapologetically rational exploration of ideas, weaving thick threads between abstract concepts and daily life. As a rule, psychotherapists have neither the mandate nor the philosophical tools to guide people through the intricacies of moral dilemmas or different understandings of the good life. Take a woman considering an abortion, for instance. In order to be of any use to her it would help to have some knowledge of the principal moral arguments, or we might end up advocating that she follows her intuition, which could be exceptionally unhelpful. A therapist may also be hampered by the assumed moral relativism that is not uncommon in the field.

But there are things that philosophical counsellors could do with learning from psychotherapy: a sensitivity to context and body language, for instance, or ways of making good use of interpersonal dynamics – within the therapeutic relationship there are clues about how a person interacts outside in the real world, and there may be much to learn from these. Then there are techniques to assist people in putting changes into practice (of course, depending on the therapy, these may be more or less useful). The ideal therapy for curious, reflective people would be a marriage of the best features of both traditions.

CONCLUSION:
THE SERENITY MANTRA

If we had to come up with a tweetable summary of universal wisdom, a strong contender would be a piece of advice that tells you nothing about what you should do. It's Reinhold Niebuhr's serenity prayer, less its first word: 'God.'

> Grant me the serenity to accept the things I cannot change,
> Courage to change the things I can,
> And wisdom to know the difference.

There are two reasons for the excision of God. First, the basic advice holds good whether you believe in God or not. Like Laplace explaining the absence of the deity from his astronomy, at least in this context there is no need of that hypothesis.

The other reason is that serenity, courage and wisdom are to be found within yourself. Removing the mention of God makes it clearer that these precious resources lie within, and therefore the prayer is best understood as a self-supplication.

It may seem odd that the serenity prayer has proved to be such a comfort and inspiration even though it doesn't tell us what to do in any specific situation. But it does something very valuable: it reminds us that at times of anguish and struggle we should shift the focus of our attention to the right questions.

If you are going through a difficult time, it's useful to ask yourself early on whether there is something you can do to change things. Easy to ask, difficult to answer. Some things are clear: you can't change the past; you can't bring the dead back to life. Beyond that, it all becomes a little more debatable.

We have strong cultural assumptions that almost anything can be changed if we want to. This faith in our ability to achieve whatever we want stands in stark contrast with the Stoics' philosophy, which was that the only thing in our control was our rational choice. Everything else – health, wealth, the people in our life – was a matter of destiny, over which we had no say whatsoever.

The Stoics may have been both too pessimistic and too optimistic. In fact things are more nuanced. On the one hand we can take steps to change our circumstances in a variety of ways. We can influence our health, for instance, by changing our diet and exercise. Of course we can only take steps, not ensure success. On the other hand, there are limits to our rational choice. There is enough research around to persuade the most sceptical of us that we are subject to an impressive array of biases, some born of our life experience, but many due simply to being human.

We should take some of the Stoic advice but aim for a more balanced position between change and acceptance. This doesn't mean we have to accept a meaningless job, a destructive relationship, or even particular character traits that we think we should make an effort to improve. It does mean accepting the flawed nature of existence, the inevitability of imperfection, the ubiquity of negative mental states. It means accepting that the role of chance in what befalls us is large, perhaps larger than anything in our control. And accepting what existential philosophers called *throwness*, or *facticity* – the fact that our freedom is limited by our finding ourselves 'thrown' in particular concrete situations that we did not choose.

The serenity prayer offers no simple test for distinguishing the changeable from the unchangeable because there is none. Which is why we need wisdom to judge whether it's realistic to change some particular situation we're in. As we have argued, practical wisdom is not an algorithmic, rule-based system, but a context-dependent art.

In any case, it has to begin with the acceptance that things are as they are. After that there are, in essence, only two possible options: either accepting that circumstances cannot change, even though attitude can; or working out what is necessary to make a change, then doing it.

But this is still not quite right. The prayer really needs a small addition to its middle line:

Courage to change the things I can and should

Some things can be changed, but the price is just too high. You may, for instance, be able to achieve an ambition only if you dedicate yourself to the task so much that you end up losing your family. Some things are just impossible, many others have a cost. It's important to think about trade-offs.

Although the serenity prayer imparts no practical advice, it reminds us to assess the most essential features of the problems and questions that face us: whether change is possible, what it requires, the need to accept or act. What's more, it does so in a way that brings to the fore the role of wisdom in the process. Finally, because it's not prescriptive about what we should actually do, it recognises the plurality of values and the autonomy of individuals to decide for themselves what the good life for them is.

We therefore commend a slightly modified version of the prayer, perhaps better described as a serenity mantra:

I will strive to accept the things I cannot change,
Change the things I can and should,
And find the wisdom to know the difference

Like most good advice, it's easier said than done, but much better said than not.

NOTES

1. Aristotle, *Nicomachean Ethics*, II, 6, trans. Roger Crisp (Cambridge University Press, 2000), p. 30.
2. Aristotle, *Nicomachean Ethics*, II, 1, trans. Roger Crisp (Cambridge University Press, 2000), p. 23.
3. Aristotle, *Nicomachean Ethics*, II, 1, trans. Roger Crisp (Cambridge University Press, 2000), p. 23.
4. Daniel Kahneman, *Thinking, Fast and Slow* (Allen Lane, 2011).
5. Aristotle, *Nicomachean Ethics*, X, 8, trans. Roger Crisp (Cambridge University Press, 2000), p. 198.
6. Aristotle, *Nicomachean Ethics*, I, 10, trans. Roger Crisp (Cambridge University Press, 2000), p. 18.
7. Aristotle, *Nicomachean Ethics*, I, 5, trans. Roger Crisp (Cambridge University Press, 2000), p. 7.
8. Gabriella Conti, Andrea Galeotti, Gerrit Mueller and Stephen Pudney, 'Popularity', ISER Working Paper Series 2009-03 (Institute for Social and Economic Research, 2009).
9. Aristotle, *Nicomachean Ethics*, VIII, 1, trans. Roger Crisp (Cambridge University Press, 2000), p. 143.
10. Aristotle, *Nicomachean Ethics*, IX, 4, trans. Roger Crisp (Cambridge University Press, 2000), p. 169.
11. Aristotle, *Nicomachean Ethics*, X, 7, trans. Roger Crisp (Cambridge University Press, 2000), p. 195.
12. Aristotle, *Nicomachean Ethics*, I, 5, trans. Roger Crisp (Cambridge University Press, 2000), p. 7.
13. John Stuart Mill, *Utilitarianism*, Ch. 11 (Fontana, 1962), pp. 258–61.
14. Émile Coué, *Self Mastery Through Conscious Autosuggestion* (American Library Service, 1922). The phrase is used several times, in the less rhyming form: 'Every day, in every respect, I'm getting better and better.'
15. Jean-Paul Sartre, *Existentialism and Humanism* (1948), in *Jean-Paul Sartre: Basic Writings*, ed. Stephen Priest (Routledge, 2001), pp. 36–7.

16. Immanuel Kant, *Groundwork of the Metaphysics of Morals* (1785), trans. Mary Gregor (Cambridge University Press, 1998). The catchy phrase is used to sum up Kant's argument, but he never used it himself.

17. Julian Baggini, 'Truth or dare: An interview with Simon Critchley', *The Philosophers' Magazine*, Issue 40, 1st Quarter 2008, pp. 74–7.

18. Julian Baggini and Jeremy Stangroom (eds), *New British Philosophy* (Routledge, 2002), p. 17.

19. Martin Seligman, *Flourish* (Nicholas Brealey, 2011), p. 13.

20. Gretchen Rubin, *The Happiness Project* (HarperCollins, 2010), p. 45.

21. HH Dalai Lama and Howard Cutler, *The Art of Happiness* (Hodder and Stoughton, 1998).

22. Martin Seligman, *Flourish* (Nicholas Brealey, 2011).

23. Daniel Gilbert, *Stumbling on Happiness* (Alfred A. Knopf, 2006).

24. Mihalyi Csikszentmihalyi, *Flow* (Harper & Row, 1992), p. 8.

25. Daniel Kahneman, *Thinking, Fast and Slow* (Allen Lane, 2011), p. 397.

26. Viktor Frankl, *Man's Search for Meaning* (Rider, 2004).

27. Bertrand Russell, *The Conquest of Happiness* (1930), (Routledge, 1993), p. 121.

28. Viktor Frankl, *Man's Search for Meaning* (Rider, 2004), p. 110.

29. Mihalyi Csikszentmihalyi, *Flow* (Harper & Row, 1992), p. 215.

30. Donald McRae, 'Interview – Tim Henman', *The Guardian*, 16 May 2005.

31. Aristotle, *Nicomachean Ethics*, I, 8, trans. Roger Crisp (Cambridge University Press, 2000), p. 12.

32. Aristotle, *Nicomachean Ethics*, I, 8, trans. Roger Crisp (Cambridge University Press, 2000), p. 196.

33. Aristotle, *Nicomachean Ethics*, X, 7, trans. Roger Crisp (Cambridge University Press, 2000), p. 46.

34. David Neal et al., 'The pull of the past: when do habits persist despite conflict with motives?', *Personality and Social*

Psychology Bulletin, November 2011.

35. See Julian Baggini, *The Ego Trick* (Granta, 2011).

36. Michel de Montaigne, 'On experience', *Essays* (Penguin, 1958), pp. 396–7.

37. See Howard V. Hong and Edna H. Hong's translations of Søren Kierkegaard, in particular *Stages on Life's Way* (1845), (Princeton University Press, 1988) and the two volumes of *Either/Or* (1843), (Princeton University Press, 1988).

38. Daniel Kahneman, *Thinking, Fast and Slow* (Allen Lane, 2011), pp. 378–90.

39. Daniel Kahneman, *Thinking, Fast and Slow* (Allen Lane, 2011), pp. 379–80.

40. David Eagleman, *Incognito* (Canongate, 2011), p. 107.

41. Aristotle, *Nicomachean Ethics*, VII, 3, trans. Roger Crisp (Cambridge University Press, 2000), p. 124.

42. Plato, *Phaedrus*, §253–255, trans. Walter Hamilton (Penguin, 1973), pp. 61–3.

43. David Hume, *A Treatise of Human Nature*, Book 2, Part III, Section III, (1739–40), (Clarendon Press, 1978), p. 415.

44. Søren Kierkegaard, *The Sickness Unto Death* (1849), trans. A. Hannay (Penguin, 1989), pp. 62–3.

45. Plato, *The Apology*, §29a, in *The Last Days of Socrates*, trans. Harold Tarrant and Hugh Tredennick (Penguin, 2003), p. 55.

46. Epicurus' principal teachings are reported in Book X of *The Lives and Opinions of the Great Philosophers* by Diogenes Laertius, and anthologised in *The Epicurus Reader*, trans. Brad Inwood and Lloyd P. Gerson (Hackett, 1994).

47. Blaise Pascal, *Pensées*, trans. A. Krailsheimer (Penguin, 1995), p. 127.

48. Paul Rusesabagina, *An Ordinary Man* (Bloomsbury, 2006), p. 260.

49. Thich Nhat Hanh, *The Miracle of Mindfulness* (Beacon Press, 1987), p. 97.

50. Antonio Damasio, *Descartes' Error* (Vintage, 2006).

51. Onora O'Neill, 'Lifeboat Earth', *Philosophy and Public Affairs*, Vol. 4, No. 3, (Spring 1975), reprinted in *Political Thought*, eds Michael Rosen and Jonathan Wolff (Oxford University

Press, 1999) pp. 304–18.

52. See Daniel Dennett, *Elbow Room* (Bradford Books, 1984) and *Consciousness Explained* (Little, Brown, 1991).

53. *Report of the APA Task Force on the Sexualization of Girls* (American Psychological Association, 2007).

54. https://implicit.harvard.edu

55. See Plato's *Republic*, trans. Robin Waterfield (Oxford University Press, 2008) and Immanuel Kant, *Critique of Pure Reason*, Second Edition (1787), trans. Norman Kemp Smith (Palgrave Macmillan, 2007).

56. Stephen P. Schwartz, 'Reason's no quitter', *The Philosophers' Magazine*, Issue 36, 4th Quarter 2006, pp. 27–30.

57. Plato, *Protagoras*, 352a1–361d6, trans. C.C.W. Taylor (Oxford University Press, 1996), pp. 54–66.

58. Russ Harris, *The Confidence Gap* (Robinson, 2011), p. 98.

59. Steven Pinker, 'A history of (non)violence', *Foreign Policy*, December 2011.

60. Paul Gilbert, *Compassion Focused Therapy* (Routledge, 2010), pp. 105–06.

61. Russ Harris, *The Confidence Gap* (Robinson, 2011), p. 102.

62. Julian Baggini, 'The Establishment Outsider: An Interview with Roger Scruton', *The Philosophers' Magazine*, Issue 42, 3rd Quarter 2008, pp. 20–30.

63. David Eagleman, *Incognito* (Canongate, 2011), p. 199.

64. See Michael Marmot, *The Status Syndrome: How Social Standing Affects Our Health and Longevity* (Holt McDougal, 2005) and Richard Wilkinson and Kate Pickett, *The Spirit Level* (Penguin, 2010).

65. Linda Hargreaves, Mark Cunningham, Anders Hansen, Donald McIntyre, Caroline Oliver and Tony Pell, *The Status of Teachers and the Teaching Profession in England: Views from Inside and Outside the Profession*, Research Report RR831A (Department for Education and Skills, 2007).

66. Martin Seligman, *Flourish* (Nicholas Brealey, 2011).

67. Frans de Waal, *Our Inner Ape* (Granta, 2005), p. 82.

68. Paul Gilbert, *The Compassionate Mind* (Constable, 2009), p. 166.

69. Bertrand Russell, *The Conquest of Happiness* (Routledge, 2000), p. 39.
70. Paul Gilbert, *Compassion Focused Therapy* (Routledge, 2010), p. 113.
71. Russ Harris, *ACT Made Simple* (New Harbinger, 2009), p. 195.
72. Dennis Greenberger and Christine Padesky, *Mind over Mood* (Guilford Press, 1995).
73. Seneca, letter xci, *Letters from a Stoic* (Penguin, 2004), p. 179.
74. Seneca, letter xxvi, *Letters from a Stoic* (Penguin, 2004), p. 71.
75. See Barbara Ehrenreich, *Smile or Die* (Granta, 2009).
76. Viktor Frankl, *Man's Search for Meaning* (Rider, 2004), pp. 139–40.
77. Matt Ridley, *The Rational Optimist* (Fourth Estate, 2010).
78. Ray Bradbury, *Golden Apples of the Sun* (Doubleday, 1953).
79. Milan Kundera, *The Unbearable Lightness of Being* (Faber and Faber, 1984), p. 8.
80. Martin Seligman, *Flourish* (Nicholas Brealey, 2011), p. 12.
81. Viktor Frankl, *Psychotherapy and Existentialism* (Washington Square Press, 1985), p. 37.
82. Viktor Frankl, *Man's Search for Meaning* (Rider, 2004), p. 115.
83. A.J. Ayer, 'The Meaning of Life', in *Life and Death*, eds Carl Levenson and Jonathan Westphal (Hackett, 1994), p. 117.
84. John Cottingham, 'The Fine, The Good, and the Meaningful', *The Philosophers' Magazine*, Issue 45, 2nd Quarter 2009, pp. 31–9. See also *Why Believe?* (Continuum, 2009).
85. See Julian Baggini, *The Ego Trick*, Chapter 4 (Granta, 2011).
86. René Descartes, *Meditations on First Philosophy*, §81, trans. John Cottingham (Cambridge University Press, 1986), p. 56.
87. *The Rule of Benedict* (Penguin Classics, 2008), p. 72.
88. Matthew Crawford, *The Case for Working with Your Hands* (Penguin, 2009), p. 68.
89. Matthew Crawford, *The Case for Working with Your Hands* (Penguin, 2009), p. 67.
90. Thich Nhat Hanh, *The Miracle of Mindfulness* (Beacon Press, 1987), p. 85.

91. Stephen Batchelor, *Buddhism Without Beliefs* (Bloomsbury, 1998), p. 6.
92. Mihalyi Csikszentmihalyi, *Flow* (Harper & Row, 1992).
93. The letter is reproduced in Martin Kusch, *Psychologism: a case study in the sociology of philosophical knowledge* (Routledge, 1995), pp. 191–2.
94. Karl Marx, 'Alienated labour', in *The Portable Karl Marx*, ed. Eugene Kamenka (Viking Penguin, 1983), p. 134.
95. Ed Diener and Louise Tay, 'The Religion Paradox: If Religion Makes People Happy, Why Are So Many Dropping Out?' *Journal of Personality and Social Psychology*, Vol. 101(6), December 2011, pp. 1278–90.
96. See 'The Stress Test' at http://www.bbc.co.uk/labuk/
97. Thomas Szasz, *The Myth of Psychotherapy* (Syracuse University Press, 1988), p. 9.
98. Sigmund Freud, *Introductory Lectures on Psychoanalysis* (Penguin, 1973), p. 41.
99. Darian Leader, 'Therapy shows us life is not neat or safe. So why judge it by those criteria?', *The Guardian*, 10 December 2010.
100. Ernesto Spinelli, *Demystifying Therapy* (PCCS Books, 2006), p. 5.
101. Ernesto Spinelli, *Practising Existential Psychotherapy* (Sage, 2007), p. 80.
102. Steven Hayes, Kirk Strosahl and Kelly Wilson, *Acceptance and Commitment Therapy* (Guilford Press, 2003), p. 6.
103. Epictetus, the Handbook, *The Discourses* (Everyman, 1995), p. 289.
104. Epictetus, the Handbook, *The Discourses* (Everyman, 1995), p. 288.
105. Pierre Hadot, *Philosophy as a Way of Life* (Blackwell, 1995).
106. Ran Lahav, 'A conceptual framework for philosophical counseling: worldview interpretation', in Lahav and Tillmans (eds), *Essays on Philosophical Counseling* (University Press of America, 1995).